The Inner-City Child

The Inner-City Child

by

Frank Riessman

HARPER & ROW, PUBLISHERS

New York · Hagerstown · San Francisco · London

FIRST EDITION

Library of Congress Cataloging in Publication Data

Riessman, Frank, date.
   The inner-city child.
   Includes index.
   1. Socially handicapped children—Education—United States. 2. Compensatory
education—United States.
   I. Title.
LC8414.R43 1976   371.9'672'0973   75–35678
ISBN 0–06–013567–0

76 77 78 79 10 9 8 7 6 5 4 3 2 1

for Cathy

Contents

Preface

When I began to write this book, I believed that I was preparing a new edition of *The Culturally Deprived Child*, which first appeared in 1962. I realized shortly that not only was the old title entirely inappropriate, but so much new material and thinking had evolved in the last decade and a half that it made more sense to write a new book. The present work, while it has continuity with the earlier book in that both stress the strengths of the inner-city child, is essentially not a new edition but a different book.

A basic theme in the present book is that it may be possible to produce a "leap" in the learning of the inner-city child, while at the same time improving the productivity and efficiency of the schools in terms of costs and benefits. The basic proposals of the book entail a better deployment of resources, particularly through the fullest utilization of educational assistants, or paraprofessionals, and children teaching children. If the strength-based approaches which I will describe are integrated meaningfully and managed effectively, we may be able to obtain much better results without increasing costs. But apart from any specific methods, it is most crucial that all educators begin to really understand the strengths of inner-city children and build their own approaches around these strengths. It is to that end that the book is directed.

I should like to express my appreciation to the members of the staff of the New Human Services Institute of Queens College, who have contributed significantly to my understanding of the strengths of the inner-city child. The assistance in this regard of William Lynch, Vivian C. Jackson, Ruth Hunter, Ethel Mingo, and Alan Gartner is particularly appreciated. The contribution of Elinor Bowles, who wrote Chapter 3, "The Strengths of the Black Culture," is central to the book as a whole, as is that of Shirley Schwartz, who coauthored Chapter 2. The assistance of David Shore is also appreciated. I should like to thank *Teachers College Record* for permitting me to use material in Chapter 5, portions of which first appeared in *Teachers College Record* in "The Strategy of Style" (March 1964), and portions of Chapter 8, which first appeared in *Teachers College Record* in "Strategies For Large-Scale Educational Reform" (February 1974), coauthored with Alan Gartner.

Others who have helped me to understand the inner-city child include Arthur Pearl, William Smith, Patricia Sexton, Kenneth Clark, S. M. Miller, and Sol Levine.

1

Overview

Since 1962, when I wrote *The Culturally Deprived Child*—the book with the very bad and misleading title—considerable changes have taken place in education in America. We now have bilingual education, open classrooms, special education for the handicapped, continuing education, external degrees, accountability, much greater community involvement, paraprofessionals, children teaching children, action learning, peer counseling, team teaching, differentiated staffing, schools without walls, preschooling, the contact curriculum, mini-schools, alternative schools, competency-based teacher evaluation, and a large number of other innovations.

Teachers seem to know a lot more about contacting youngsters via the use of games, role playing, and films, with less emphasis on standardized lectures and demonstrations. But all this has not produced, by almost any indicator one chooses to use, significant improvements in the learning of inner-city youngsters.[1] The question is why.

I think in the last analysis there are four overall reasons:

1. Educators continue to use, whether implicitly or explic-

---

1. I shall use the term "inner-city" child throughout to refer essentially to children of the urban poor, largely Black and minority children. The problems and strengths of other inner-city children, such as Puerto Ricans and Chicanos, are similar in many ways, but are different regarding their language and cultural traditions. Low-income Appalachian children have significant similarities with the inner-city child, but again there are differences related to their rural traditions and life.

1

itly, a basic compensatory model; that is, they assume that inner-city youngsters are inadequate and need all kinds of *special help to make them like middle-class children.* No matter what teachers do, the message the child hears is: I am inadequate, deficient, missing something. The educators do not lead from the strengths, the positive culture, the coping abilities, the cognitive styles of these youngsters; they do not build their methods, consciously and fully, around these strengths, although many specific approaches that are strength-based have emerged and we shall discuss some of them in the course of this book. But there is no overall design or pattern integrating these strength-based approaches, and in fact, a new intensive compensatory approach has emerged, as we shall see.

2. While the great emphasis on teaching has led in some ways to the improvement of the teacher's ability to contact youngsters, most teachers *do not know how to move beyond the contact stage* to higher stages of learning and development. Consequently, they keep the children at this contact level, often entertaining them rather than helping them learn how to learn or developing in them an understanding of the structure of the subject matter.

3. The improvement of teachers has not led to the improvement of the management of the educational system. I believe principals may be much more fundamental in the improvement of learning and we need to concentrate much more on them.

4. Finally, we have not developed sound organizational and management strategies, so that good programs and strength-based approaches that have emerged in various demonstrations can be carried over and institutionalized in the system as a whole. (This issue is discussed in Chapter 8.)

This book is directed toward providing a better basis for a large-scale leap in the learning of inner-city children. In essence, the argument is that if we understand the strengths, the coping skills, the positive culture, the genuine verbal ability of these youngsters and their families, we will be able to institute a rounded strength-based educational strategy, rather than the compensatory scenario that has dominated the scene, which assumes as a basic tenet that the child is inadequate. Strength-based approaches, of course, have been developed throughout the last decade—children teaching children, various types of contact methods, schools without walls, the use of neighborhood community paraprofessionals who understand the background and culture of the inner-city child, and many more. The problem is that these approaches are neither developed fully, nor self-consciously, nor in an integrated design. Rather they have evolved haphazardly, anarchically, frequently mixed together with highly compensatory approaches; nor have they been well organized and managed.

Underlying all these difficulties is the fact that educators in general still do not believe that inner-city children have good verbal ability and an enormous number of strengths. Consequently I will devote considerable attention to providing the underlying rationale for the strength-based approaches, and will discuss first the verbal ability of inner-city people, then the myths about their intelligence along with the whole IQ controversy, followed by a discussion of the strengths of their culture, and their cognitive style.

The last portion of the book is devoted to educational strategies, moving toward an authentic accountability that is concerned with the learning of children as evaluated by a variety of indicators, rather than the acquiring by teachers of competencies which may or may not be related to the learning of children (Compentency-Based Teacher Education).

But the failure of education with regard to inner-city children, and really all children in the last decade, is not simply due to compensatory and other inadequate educational approaches. While this book directs itself mainly to the education agenda— that is, what can be done within the field of education itself— it has to be remembered that the extra-educational sources of the difficulty, which reside in the society, must be dealt with. No amount of improved education will be fully meaningful to inner-city youngsters if they do not have the prospect—a realistic prospect—of decent, useful work.

Only a *full-employment economy,* in which meaningful jobs are available for everyone who wishes to work, can provide the basis for the fullest improvement of the learning of the youngsters. Moreover, in a society that has a declining percentage of jobs in manufacturing and goods production, opportunities will have to be created in the service fields, such as education itself, but also in health, recreation, mental health, welfare, and so on. Thus there needs to be a shift in expenditures in our economy, particularly from the military sectors into the service and educational areas, rather than the current decrease in the proportion of funds that are expended in these areas and the concomitant maintenance or increase of military expenditures. While this book does not address these questions, they have to be constantly considered as a backdrop to the entire discussion, otherwise we will sound grandiose and unreal in endeavoring to make needed educational changes to improve the learning of youngsters.

Education itself is a very important sphere for the improvement of this learning and must be considered in its own right; but it must be constantly remembered that the larger societal context and the economy have also to be changed, otherwise we will have the one-sided cultural revolution of the sixties—or rather the revolutionary aspirations of the sixties—without the needed economic and structural changes. In essence, then, we disagree fundamentally with John Dewey: we do not live in a "school-centered" society, we learn in society-centered schools, and these schools in the last analysis reflect what is going on in that society. Unless that society is restructured, there are fundamental limits to the improvements that can be produced in the educational field itself.

A CULTURAL APPROACH: CULTURE VERSUS ENVIRONMENT

It is easy to say that we must understand the culture of inner-city groups. Most people would agree. The question is, what do we mean by the culture of the inner city? Some people seem to think that the culture of a group is equivalent to its environment. Therefore, the culture of lower socioeconomic groups is seen to include inadequate housing, limited access to jobs, and the like. I prefer to distinguish between the environment, or conditions of life, of a group, and the culture of that group. I conceive the latter to be the methods that have evolved for coping with the conditions of life. Thus "culture" would include the traditions, values, and mores of a specific group.

Along with customs and traditions, there are the institutions, the structures, the methods of organization of the people involved. The storefront church, the civil rights movement, the extended family, the neighborhood club, are illustrative here in relation to inner-city people.

I view culture, then, as an effort to cope with the surrounding environment. Many of the coping techniques may be ineffective, of course, but only if they are seen in terms of an effort to grapple with the milieu will they be properly understood. If we fail to see the struggle, the attempts to combat the difficult environment, and instead seize upon the failures, we will not understand the behavior of the poor, or at best will see it only one-sidedly.

Educators must understand the culture of inner-city groups. This is not the same thing as recognizing the economic difficulties and general life conditions of the poor. Most informed people are cognizant of the "deprived" side of the picture.

It is natural enough for educators to stress the liabilities of the underprivileged. These are the things that the teacher is confronted with all the time. From the teacher's point of view, the inner-city child clearly is not happy in school, does not read well, appears unmotivated, is antagonistic to the teachers, possesses few well-formulated career plans. These are the things that are easiest to see because they are on the surface. To see the strengths and positive struggles requires a deeper, more penetrating look.

Many people see only the negative environmental conditions that surround the poor, and they believe that this is the culture. They feel that it is democratic and liberal to "accept" this culture as just another way of life. But understanding of this culture must include a genuine appreciation of the positive aspects that have arisen out of the effort, however insufficient at times, to cope with the difficult environment.

This is different from the standard view, which, by accenting deprivation, emphasizes weakness. In fact, one of the great difficulties with formulations like "culturally deprived," "disadvantaged," "culturally handicapped," "impoverished," and the like, is that they connote inadequacy, rather than a rounded picture of the culture, which would have to include strengths as well as deficiencies. The view presented here also constrains against snobbery and patronization. It is difficult to patronize someone whose strengths you are well aware of. To the extent that genuine cultural understanding takes place, there will be improvement in rapport in the classroom, the guidance office, and the Parent-Teacher Association.

There are at least two ways in which a cultural approach can aid the teacher. One has to do with the social-emotional relationship between teacher and child; the other is more directly concerned with the way subject matter can best be taught.

A sound cultural understanding should enable the teacher to establish a much better relationship with the child who has grown antagonistic toward the school. Through an empathic understanding of the culture, the teacher can begin to see why some children become hostile and what they expect of the teacher. Teachers will come to learn how they can utilize the strengths and styles of inner-city children. They will come to understand why the child needs not love but respect. And finally, they will be able to interpret in a new light much of the behavior that appears negative.

EDUCATION FOR WHAT?

I do not intend to romanticize or idealize poverty or the poor. There is no question that poor people suffer as a result of their environment in terms of their housing, health, the services they receive, income and so on. But they also struggle with this environment, are angered by it, sometimes organize against it, and they develop a culture and institutions to deal with it. If they did not struggle with the sources of their inequality and discrimination and their inadequate environment, the poor would have to depend entirely on outside help—help from others whose conditions are not the same, and whose self-interests are not the same. While these groups, liberals and others, may be important allies in the struggle against poverty, they cannot be the leaders of it nor the main force. Whites did not lead the civil rights movement, although they were important allies in it, and middle-class people did not lead the welfare rights movement, although again they were useful allies. It is essentially the exploited and oppressed people themselves who provide the main motion for the change in their conditions. Thus I endeavor to search out the positive threads, the sources of motion within the victims of oppression, rather than to blame the victims by one-sidedly emphasizing their negative environment.

My aim in education is *not* to have the poor think and behave like the present-day middle class, because the middle class has too many defects, as current criticism indicates. Middle-class life is characterized by much alienation, competiveness, and dehumanization. My aim is for the poor to become nonpoor, and in the process to help change society so that all of us—poor and middle class—may become more complete human beings. In essence, what I am saying is that the poor are not going to become nonpoor without changing the whole society in the process—without the redistribution of income and wealth, which will require basic structural changes.

Reading and education in general are important tools for reaching this objective. These tools *do not belong to any class;* that is, reading is not middle-class, nor is learning and general education. Education is a necessary, though not a sufficient, condition for producing needed societal change. It cannot remain the private property of the upper class. Thus, while I do not agree with the Dewey dictum of a school-centered society, in which the school is the pivotal element in social transformation, I do see education as a revolutionary essential, and attempts to roll back the clock such as cutting expenditures in education and discouraging people from obtaining higher education as highly reactionary. That educational credentials have been misused as criteria for obtaining jobs is no reason to discard education or to underestimate its potential role as an instrument for social change. On the other hand, people acquire education in the hope that it will help them in the job world, and to the extent that there are no jobs at the end of the educational rainbow, considerable disillusionment with education results.

Finally, it must be recognized that there are powerful limits on our potential for changing education in a society characterized by inequality, racism, planned unemployment, exploitation, and environmental waste. In the sixties, progressive forces made the error of urging a one-sided cultural revolution, one that was concerned with changing interpersonal relations, education, and the like, but overlooked the need for basic economic and political change.

In the seventies we may be coming to learn that we cannot simply have a cultural revolution, that we need also an economic and political revolution if we are to have serious social transformation and if education is to be most beneficial.

In essence, then, my answer to the question Education for what? is: Education for equality, for social change, for self-development, for overcoming a life of waste and alienation, and as a tool for a more meaningful understanding of the world, and the action that flows from such an understanding.

2

Is the Inner-City Child Nonverbal?

It would be easy enough to assume that inner-city children are essentially nonverbal or verbally deficient. They consistently lag behind their more advantaged age-mates on standardized tests of verbal performance, reading achievement, and the like. Such evidence, however, may reveal more about the inadequacies in our educational methods with poor, minority children than it does about their presumed verbal deficiencies. A more careful examination of the issues and the research garnered by linguists over the past decade seriously calls into question the belief that the poor are nonverbal or verbally deficient. Because verbal behavior is so important, it is necessary to examine the ideas surrounding the assumption of verbal inadequacy as well as try to specify the exact nature of the verbal repertoire of inner-city people.

One reason for the conception of the inner-city child as nonverbal, verbally deficient, or verbally undeveloped or restricted has as its basis the kind of research gathered from typical testing situations, rather than more natural settings. Labov's linguistic research among Harlem youth[1] demonstrates the importance of the subtle sociolinguistic forces operating in the interaction between the inner-city child and the adult. He relates the story of a conversation with eight-year-old Leon, who responded to most questions with "I don't know," "No," and

This chapter was jointly written with Shirley Schwartz.

1. William Labov, "Academic Ignorance and Black Intelligence," *Atlantic Monthly* 299, no. 6 (June 1972): 59–67.

"Nope," even when interviewed by a skilled empathic adult. Leon was reacting to the "asymmetrical" power relationship with the adult interviewer. There was a dramatic change, however, when he was subsequently interviewed in a more comfortable situation—a party atmosphere in which potato chips were provided, his best friend, Gregory, was present, taboo topics were introduced, and the interviewer got down on the floor of Leon's room, minimizing the height differential and implicit imbalance in the power relations between them. The transcript of this interview shows that:

> The "non-verbal" Leon is now competing actively for the floor; Gregory and Leon talk to each other as much as they do to the interviewer. The monosyllabic speaker who had nothing to say about anything and could not remember what he did yesterday has disappeared. Instead, we have two boys who have so much to say that they keep interrupting each other. . . .[2]

In role-playing sessions one can observe that the verbal performance of inner-city children is markedly improved not only during the role-playing but also in the discussion period following the sessions. When talking about some action they have seen, inner-city children verbalize freely. In the middle-class adult world of school, clinic, or research setting, they usually do not verbalize well in response to words alone. These children express themselves more readily when reacting to things they can see and do. Ask an inner-city youngster what he doesn't like about school or the teacher and you may very well get an abbreviated, inarticulate reply. But have a group of youngsters act out a school scene in which someone plays the teacher and you will discover a stream of verbal consciousness that is almost impossible to shut off.

In order for the child's verbal behavior to be freely expressed and adequately assessed, it must be done in a setting in which the child is comfortable, with materials and people with whom he or she is familiar, and using techniques congruent with his or her own verbal style. Of course, this is basic to good testing technique with all children; however, these principles typically have been abused with low-income children. The result is that they often do behave as if they were nonverbal,

2. Ibid., p. 159.

fulfilling the language demands of an adult-centered interaction passively and with minimal comment.[3] However, when, the child's verbal behavior is expressed in a more naturalistic setting and studied with more sophisticated techniques, the verbally deficient child disappears. Instead, we see a child who participates fully in a highly verbal culture. As Labov indicates:

> We see a child bathed in verbal stimulation from morning to night. We see many speech events which depend upon the competitive exhibitions of verbal skills: singing, sounding, toasts, rifting, louding—a whole range of activities in which the individual gains status through the use of language.[4]

Some years ago the Institute for Developmental Studies, under Martin Deutsch, conducted a series of investigations of the language patterns of inner-city children:

> In our own study, we encountered interesting surprises. We assumed that the inner-city child, when confronted with a word-association task, will respond in a somewhat stereotyped or rigid manner; instead we find that both first and fifth grade inner city children give rich associations.[5]

Deutsch's staff utilized a novel technique to elicit the child's "spontaneous language," which in the case of the inner-city child seems to be more developed than might be expected. The child is presented with a large toy clown; the clown's nose lights up when the child talks, and the child is free to choose his topic. The clown's nose fails to light up when the child is silent, and the child is told this means "The clown is sad." Inner-city children were much more verbally expressive in this situation than in the usual classroom or research surroundings.

Other findings reported by Deutsch are:

1. Inner-city children appear to be poor in the use of verbs, but much better with descriptive adjectives.

3. The importance of social factors in testing the verbal behavior of inner-city people has, of course, more than anecdotal support, as seen, for instance, in Joyce Dickie and Susana Bagur's recent review of the research: "Considerations for the Study of Language in Young Low-Income Minority Group Children," *Merrill-Palmer Quarterly* 18, no. 4 (1972): 25–38.

4. Labov, op cit., p. 160.

5. Report no. 5 from the Institute for Developmental Studies, New York, 1961.

2. Inner-city children seem to understand more language than they speak (their "receptive" linguistic ability is much better than their "expressive" language).
3. Inner-city children demonstrate a surprising ability for fantasy (as seen in the clown situation).
4. Inner-city children express themselves best in spontaneous, unstructured situations.

Irving Taylor, formerly on the staff of the Institute for Developmental Studies, has some novel ideas about the untapped creative potential of inner-city children. He believes that these children are not nearly so nonverbal as is generally thought. He says that they use words in a different way and are not as dependent on words for their sole form of communication, but that nevertheless they are imaginative at the verbal level.[6]

Taylor finds on word-association tests that inner-city children give responses that are often less conventional, more unusual, original, and independent. They seem to be more flexible and visual with language. For example, to the word "stone," inner-city children are more willing to give associations such as "solid" and "hard," responses that encompass the perceptual qualities of the object. They are also more likely to say "throw it in a lake," "chop things up with it." Middle-class children restrict their associations more to standard synonyms like "rock," "pebble." Inner-city children include these words also —they know that they "belong" with "stone"—but they are freer in including other words.

Taylor feels that inner-city individuals are not as restricted by verbal forms of communication, but tend to permit language to interact more with nonverbal means of communication, such as gestures and pictures. This interaction with other kinds of communication gives them the potential for "breaking through the language barrier"; they are not forced to think in terms of the structure of language, as are so many people. They are less word-bound. Taylor believes that this wide range of associations by inner-city people indicates a freer use of language, which may be an important attribute of one type of creativity. He contends that not only do studies of creative people indicate that they have greater "semantic flexibility," but also that they respond well to visual, tactile, and kinesthetic cues. In general,

6. Personal communication from Irving Taylor.

their nonaural senses seem to be especially acute. Taylor notes that this pattern resembles the mental approach of the inner-city child in many respects.

There is another conception of the nonverbal, verbally deficient inner-city child, however, that relates not so much to whether the child talks a lot or a little, but rather to the presumption that when he or she does talk, the language used is "inadequate," "impoverished" or simply "bad" English. However, linguists such as Stewart,[7] Dillard,[8] Labov,[9] Baratz and Baratz,[10] and others point out that the poor possess a wealth of verbal skills and a well-ordered, highly developed language, but this language is different from the mainstream language, the standard English of our schools.

While it is obvious that the native tongue of Puerto Ricans, Chicanos, Haitians, and other foreign-language people differs from standard English, the linguists demonstrate that the primary language of inner-city blacks—variously called nonstandard English, Black English Vernacular, or Black English—also differs in some fundamental ways from the school standard. (We do not mean to imply, however, that there is a perfect analogy between Black English and a foreign language.) What may appear to the middle-class speaker or listener as "bad" English is, as we shall see, actually a highly organized linguistic system with a long history and a complex and coherent structure of vocabulary, grammar, and pronunciation all its own.[11]

7. William Stewart, "Urban Negro Speech: Sociolinguistic Factors Affecting English Teaching," in *Social Dialects and Language Learning*, ed. R. Shuy (Champaign, Ill.: National Council of Teachers of English, 1964): 70–73.

8. J. L. Dillard, *Black English: Its History and Usage in the United States* (New York: Vintage Books, 1973).

9. Labov, op. cit., p. 62.

10. Stephen Baratz and Joan Baratz, "Early Childhood Intervention: The Social Science Base of Institutional Racism," *Harvard Educational Review* 40 (1970): 29–50.

11. In contrast, there is the second "language" of many middle-class educated speakers that ostensibly diverges from the mainstream standard; for example, the jargon of cocktail party analysts ("Her trouble is, she's repressed her hostility") or perhaps of *belles lettres* ("It was a Hemingway"). But this second "language" is essentially the same as the primary standard English of its speakers. The specialized words and phrases are used with same English syntax and more than likely said with the same "network standard" pronunciation. Unlike Black English, it is not a separate linguistic system.

At this point one may ask what difference it makes whether we say that the language of the poor is a different linguistic system or simply an impoverished, "bad" English. Inner-city children still have to achieve competence and facility with standard English in order to negotiate successfully with the mainstream culture. But the conception of the verbal functioning of the poor is, in fact, crucial to our vision of educational strategy and to our views of the children themselves. As we shall see, it does indeed make a difference. If poor Blacks, white ethnics, Puerto Ricans, Chicanos, and others are viewed as linguistically impoverished or restricted, then educational strategy demands that we "compensate" for these deficiencies by "filling the vacuum," so to speak. On the other hand, if the poor come to school already equipped with a systematic though different linguistic system (which has many positive features), then we may build on the verbal strengths the children already possess. Moreover, to perceive the child as being verbally impoverished is not only incorrect, it is dangerous. Children who are viewed as nonverbal may very likely comply with our expectations of them; and we may then demand less of them, starting a vicious cycle of educational failure.

VERBAL DEFICIENCY OR VERBAL DIFFERENCE?

It is necessary at this point to examine in greater detail some of the theoretical views surrounding the verbal functioning of the poor, since these ideas have important implications for educational strategy. The most extreme view, formulated by Bereiter and Engelmann, maintains that the poor have no language at all, are verbally underdeveloped, and essentially nonverbal.[12] Another idea—equally fallacious, though more sophisticated—acknowledges that inner-city people have a language, but maintains that it is a restricted or inferior one that leads to or is caused by cognitive deficits. Moreover, the presumed "verbal-cognitive deficits" are attributed to inadequacy in the early

12. C. Bereiter and S. Engelmann, *Teaching Disadvantaged Children in the Preschool* (Englewood Cliffs, N. J.: Prentice-Hall, 1968); and C. Bereiter et al., "An Academically Oriented Preschool for Culturally Deprived Children," in *Pre-school Education Today*, ed. R. Hechinger (New York: Doubleday, 1966).

mother-child verbal interaction (Bernstein;[13] Jensen;[14] Deutsch;[15] and John[16]).

In contrast, there is the "verbal difference" view of the linguists—one that we share—which maintains that inner-city people have a different language and verbal style, but this difference does not constitute inferiority. In fact, there are positive strengths in the linguistic and verbal difference (Stewart;[17] Dillard;[18] Labov ;[19] Baratz and Baratz;[20] Vuke-

13. Basil Bernstein, "Elaborated and Restricted Codes: Their Social Origins and Some Consequences," in *Communication and Culture*, ed. A. F. Smith (New York: Holt, Rinehart, and Winston, 1966), pp. 427–41. _____, "Linguistic Codes, Hesitation Phenomena and Intelligence," *Language and Speech*, no. 5 (1962): 31–46. _____, "Social Class, Linguistic Codes and Grammatical Elements," *Language and Speech*, no. 5 (1962): 221–40.

14. A. R. Jensen, "Social Class and Verbal Learning," in *Social Class, Race, and Psychological Development*, eds. Martin Deutsch et. al. (New York: Holt, Rinehart, and Winston, 1968), p. 96.

15. Martin Deutsch, "The Role of Social Class in Language Development and Cognition," *American Journal of Orthopsychiatry*, no. 25 (1965): 78–88. _____, "The Disadvantaged Child and the Learning Process," in *Education in Depressed Areas*, ed. A. H. Passow (New York: Columbia University Press, 1963), pp. 163–79.

16. Vera John, "The Intellectual Development of Slum Children: Some Preliminary Findings," *American Journal of Orthopsychiatry*, no. 33 (1963); 813–22. Vera John and Leo Goldstein, "The Social Context of Language Acquisition," *Merrill-Palmer Quarterly*, no. 10 (1964): 265–75.

17. Stewart, op. cit. _____ "Foreign Language Teaching Methods in Quasi-Foreign Language Situation," in *Non-Standard Speech and the Teaching of English*, ed. W. A. Stewart (Washington, D.C.: Center for Applied Linguistics, 1965), pp. 16–24. _____, "Sociolinguistic Factors in the History of American Negro Dialects," *Florida Foreign Language Reporter*, no. 5 (1967): 11–29. _____, "Continuity and Change in American Negro Dialects," *Florida Foreign Language Reporter*, no. 6 (1968): 3–14.

18. Dillard, op. cit. _____, *All-American English* (New York: Random House, 1975).

19. Labov, op. cit. _____, "Stages in Acquisition of Standard English," in *Social Dialects and Language Learning*, ed. R. Shuy (Champaign, Ill.: National Council of Teachers of English, 1964), pp. 3–12. _____, "Negro Nonstandard and Standard English: Same or Different Deep Structure?" *Orbis*, no. 18 (1969): 74–91. William Labov et al., *A Study of the Nonstandard English of Negro and Puerto Rican Speakers in New York City: Final Report*, U.S. Office of Education Cooperative Research Project No. 3288, mimeographed (New York: Columbia University Press, 1968).

20. Baratz and Baratz, op. cit. Joan Baratz, "A Bidialectical Task for Determining Language Proficiency in Economically Disadvantaged Children," *Child Development* 40, no. 3 (1969): 889–901.

lich;[21] and others). Furthermore, the glib assumption
of verbal deficiency in the mother-child interaction is questioned by the linguists.[22]

The verbal-deficit view has been greatly influenced by the
ideas of Basil Bernstein, a British sociologist. Bernstein con-
tended that the middle class possessed an "elaborated" code of
speech, while working-class speech was essentially "restricted."
He suggested that these varying characteristics of speech give
a direction to feeling and thinking. The code of the middle class
is said to permit complex conceptual thought and differentiated
experience, whereas the code of the lower working class is said
to limit the kind of thinking and the type of stimuli to which the
individual can respond.[23]

Considering his influence, it is surprising to find that Bernstein based his theoretical views on only one poorly designed
study of a very small sample in which he analyzed the speech
of English adolescent boys. The sample consisted of working-
class messengers and middle-class prep school students. The
study itself, based on tape recordings of the boys' discussions of
capital punishment, was poorly designed. The sample was extremely small; from the original sample of 61 working-class boys
and 45 middle-class boys, 5 subgroups of 3 to 5 members were
used. In total, therefore, the actual sample was only 22, 12
working-class boys and 10 middle-class boys. The topic selected
was of no great relevance to either group of boys. And most
important, the two groups were given unequal treatment. The
working-class boys had two extra practice sessions, but as
Cazden so aptly pointed out,[24] the extra practice did not work
in their favor but in favor of Bernstein's bias. This paradoxical
result was a product of the operational measure of the "restricted code," namely, greater predictability—less hesitancy
and more fluency in speech. This, in turn, was based on the
assumption that hesitations in speech are related to the sym-

21. Carol Vukelich, "The Language of the Disadvantaged Child: A Deficient Language?" EDRS, Ed# 975 097 (1973).

22. William Labov, "The Logic of Nonstandard English," *Atlantic
Monthly*, op. cit., p. 63.

23. Bernstein, op. cit.

24. Courtney B. Cazden, "Subcultural Differences in Child Language: An
Inter-Disciplinary Review," *Merrill-Palmer Quarterly* 12, no.3 (1966): 185–219.

bolic dimension, whereas fluent or glib speech is more habitual, more predictable, and less conceptual. It seems likely that the extra practice given only to the working-class group might increase their fluency, hence, by definition, increase their use of the "restricted code."

Nevertheless, Bernstein's theory was accepted with wide enthusiasm and applied to the linguistic situation of poor Blacks and other minorities in the U.S. This occurred because his theory fit into the standard testing format (e.g., middle-class university setting rather than ghetto neighborhood); meshed with the data of the middle-class researcher as he or she tested children who, like Leon, were initially defensive and nonverbal; and, finally, seemed to explain lower-class language. All this occurred, of course, before the linguistic studies clearly showed that Black English Vernacular has a structure, and is a separate dialect, not a "code" of English.

Bereiter and Engelmann's "nonverbal" hypothesis, influenced by Bernstein, is based on an interpretation of the restricted code.[25] This interpretation leads them to an educational program for preschool inner-city children that assumes that the children use "a basically non-logical mode of expressive behavior," in effect, "no language at all."[26] The children's Black English sentences (for example, "Me got juice.") are taken as evidence that the children are incapable of making any kind of statement. Bereiter and Engelmann's educational program consists of drilling the children with standard English sentence structure.

The empirical evidence used to support the conception of a verbally deficient child is the relationship, found in the research, between social class and performance on verbal tasks. In both the standardized school tests and the research settings, however, the criterion for success on verbal tasks is generally the middle-class norm, standard English. When such specific criteria as "mean sentence length" and "number of grammatical errors" are used (as in the Cloze technique),[27] then obviously a Black English–speaking child who says, for instance, "He

25. Bereiter and Engelmann, op. cit.
26. Bereiter et al., op. cit., pp. 112–13.
27. Deutsch, 1965, op. cit., is an example of a study that uses these criteria.

goin'," will not fare as well as his middle-class age-mate who says, "He is going." The research demonstrating a supposed generalized language deficiency, then, is actually demonstrating the performance level of inner-city children in another language, middle-class language. (In this regard, the attempt to develop a dialect-fair test of language ability is a good idea, though the actual design of a truly fair test appears quite complex and problematic.)[28]

There is no questioning the fact that inner-city children *do* need help in improving their verbal skill in reading and writing in standard English and should master formal writing, public communication, etc. But that is an *educational* issue, which must be clearly separated from the issue of the verbal capabilities of these children. In this regard, the linguistic research overwhelmingly demonstrates that inner-city children are as competent in their own primary language as more advantaged children are in their native tongue.

As an illustration, Baratz tested inner-city Black children and middle-class children on their ability to repeat utterances in Black English and in standard English. The ability to repeat utterances is often used in language studies of young children to assess their level of verbal competence. She found that both groups of children were equally competent in their verbal behavior and exhibited similar behavior when confronted with sentences outside their own dialect. The middle-class children repeated the standard English sentences better than the inner-city children; but the inner-city children repeated the Black English sentences better than their more advantaged peers.[29]

Baratz also analyzed the language samples of Black Head Start nursery school children. She found that many utterances that could be classified as "restricted," using standard English as the criterion, would have to be more legitimately classified as the mature, adult form using Black English as the criterion. (For example, an utterance like "When your sister come home don't let her see nothin'" in standard English is "restricted," but in Black English follows the syntax of the mature form.) The inner-city children are not, therefore, at a retarded or underdeveloped or deficient level of verbal functioning; rather they

28. Cazden, op. cit.
29. Baratz, op. cit.

have mastered a language that in their environment is completely functional for the communication of ideas and feelings.

BLACK ENGLISH

Is there really such a language as Black English? Black English is the dialect spoken almost exclusively by inner-city Black Americans. When such statements as, "I ask Kevin do he know how to play basketball," or "I can skate better than Lewis and I be only eight," are said by a young child, there is no problem identifying the child as Black and poor. Of course, many Blacks speak (and read and write) only the standard English of school. And many Blacks are clearly bidialectical, switching from the vernacular of the streets to the language of school depending upon the situation, and incidentally indicating great verbal facility. Many whites who live in close proximity to Blacks in urban ghettos, especially Puerto Rican children who have Black friends, also use Black English, in addition to their own native tongue.

A language or dialect does not attach itself magically or genetically to skin color. Instead, Black English developed and is developing as a result of regular social and historical factors in the encounter between African and European cultures. The language as it is today is traceable specifically to the interaction between Blacks and whites in the South in early American history, to survivals from African languages, and to the need for a common language.[30] The language of disadvantaged Blacks— Creolized, Africanized, and Southernized English—was passed down from generation to generation, learned and mastered by Black children in the same way that children everywhere learn and master their native tongue.

Walter Murray[31] reminds us that in everyday conversation inner-city people demonstrate a language that is often rich in

30. ". . . [The slaveholder's] rule that forbade speaking in African tongues went hand-in-hand with the rule that forbade the assembly of slaves at any other than pre-arranged, supervised times. After all, the slaves who could speak together, could plot rebellion together and in the earliest years of slavery, fear of rebellion was uppermost in every owner's mind." Karyn J. Taylor, "Linguistic Blues: Black English from a Black Perspective," unpublished honors thesis, 1976.

31. Personal communication from Walter Murray.

simile and analogy. This is evident in their use of slang and
cursing. The vocabulary of inner-city groups is famous for its use
of imaginative nicknames and shortenings. The word "oreo,"
for example, describes a Black person who is white (in values,
ideology, etc.) on the inside and black only in skin color.[32]

A large proportion of the new words that have become part
of the mainstream language are said to have had their origin
among inner-city Blacks. Some of the words have been used by
Black musicians and then adopted by the hip young whites who
have been much influenced by the culture of Black people. Such
expressive words as "jazz" (African in origin), "soul," "funky,"
"gig," and even such relatively precise musical expressions as
"going through rough changes" are illustrative of this process.
The colorful, metaphoric word power of Blacks is also seen in the
perpetually changing hip vernacular of the street: "bread"
(money); "cool it" (take it easy); "dig" (understand); "far out"
(fantastic); "foxy" (attractive); "tough" (nice); "wheels" (car); etc.
Most of these words are already dated and no longer form part of
the language of inner-city people. In fact, hip words such as these
appear to be the most inventive and changeable aspect of Black
English: as soon as they get picked up by the youth culture and
the media, and adopted into the establishment language, they
tend to disappear from the street vernacular (and in time from
the establishment language as well) in favor of fresher terms.

Many, if not most, of the words in Black English Vernacular
and standard English are in fact identical. But even where they
are identical, words in the two dialects often have important
connotative or grammatical differences. The identity of many
of the words in Black English and standard English is probably
the root of the misconception that Black English is "bad" English. For example, when a Black child says, "They mine," he
or she is obviously using words that are the same in standard

32. Many Chinese people similarly use the word "banana" to describe a
person who is yellow on the outside, but white on the inside. Another example
of an evocative, metaphoric term comes from Puerto Rican Spanish: the word
is "salsa," which is used to describe modern Latin music such as Eddie Pal-
mieri's. "Salsa" comes from *salsa picante*, which is Spanish for "hot sauce," and
in describing Latin music it evokes both the idea of hot, pungent sounds and
the mix of African, Carribbean, and North American musical influences that go
into the music.

English. As a consequence, it appears as if he or she is not using the language properly. In actuality, the child is speaking in perfectly grammatical Black English, applying a syntactical rule of his or her primary language that carries contraction one step further to delete the connective *'re*. (Russian, Hungarian, and Arabic similarly do not have a present connecting link between the subject and its predicate.) The child is not making a random error, but rather is applying a rule that requires knowledge of the grammar of his or her own language.

The clarification of the linguists that the primary language of inner-city Blacks is not a collection of capricious errors is revealed most clearly in their analyses of its grammar. By grammar is meant the rules and syntax of a language.[33]

33. Here are some of the major features of Black English grammar.
(1) Verb tense is optional in Black English, unlike standard English where it is obligatory: "The boy *carried* the dog dish to the house and he *put* some dog food in it and *bring* it out and *called* his dog"; "I *see* it yesterday."
(2) Different negators, however, are used to show present and past tenses "He *not* workin' " and "I *don'* see it" indicate the present tense, but "I *ain'* see it" marks the past tense.
(3) Whereas verb tense is optional, the ongoing, intermittent, or static quality of an action must be noted. The word *be* is used (replacing *is, am,* or *are* in standard English) to indicate action of long duration, repeated action, generality, or an existential state: "He be workin' "; "She be with us"; "He be foolin' around." "He be waitin' for me every night" is grammatically different from "He waitin' for me right now." The lack of the word *be* in the latter indicates that it is momentary action; it would be *incorrect* to say "He be waitin' for me right now."
(4) The double negative is used in Black English: "He don't know nothin' "; "It ain' no use me working' so hard." (The double negative is also found in Spanish, French, Hungarian, and Russian and in informal standard English.)
(5) The double subject is found in some constructions: "John he live in Detroit" (Here is an instance where Black English is more redundant than English.)
(6) Possession is not marked by *'s* but by juxtaposition: "Ray sister."
(7) Pluralization is indicated nonredundantly after a numeral or other expression which clearly shows plurality: "Many million dollar"; "a whole lotta song."
(8) The pronoun system differs from English: "Her paitin' wif a spoon"; "Me help you?"
(9) Conditionality is expressed without the word if, sometimes *iffen* is used in its place: "I don't know can he go"; "Even a man get rich, he still pay taxes"; "She get the doctor iffen she think he real bad off."
For a more extensive treatment of the subject, the reader should see Dillard, *Black English,* especially Chapter 2, "On the Structure of Black English," pp. 39–72. The Summary of some of the features of Black English grammar and the

The following table summarizes the grammatical rules of Black English:[34]

COMPARISON OF GRAMMATICAL RULES OF STANDARD ENGLISH
AND BLACK ENGLISH

Variable	Standard English	Black English
Linking verb	He is going.	He goin'.
Possessive marker	John's cousin.	John cousin.
Plural marker	I have five cents.	I got five cent.
Subject expression	John lives in New York.	John he live in New York.
Verb form	I drank the milk.	I drunk the milk.
Past marker	Yesterday he walked home.	Yesterday he walk home.
Verb agreement	He runs home.	He run home.
	She has a bicycle.	She have a bicycle.
	They were going home.	They was goin' home.
Future form	I will go home.	I'ma go home.
"If" construction	I asked if he did it.	I ask did he do it.
Negation	I don't have any.	I don't got none.
	He didn't go.	He ain't go.
Indefinite article	I want an apple.	I want a apple.
Pronoun form	We have to do it.	Us got to do it.
	His book.	He book.
	Their book.	They book.
Preposition	He is over at his friend's house	He is over to his friend house.
	He teaches at the high school.	He teach the high school.
Statement	He is here.	He be here.
Contradiction	No, he isn't.	No, he don't.

As a distinct linguistic system, is it still possible that Black English is an inferior or restricted or deficient one? The linguists point out that every linguistic system is capable of communicating meanings, and expressing feelings and abstractions;

---

illustrative phrases and sentences that follow in the text are based, in good measure, on that source.

34. Joan C. Baratz and Roger W. Shuy, *Teaching Black Children to Read* (Washington D.C.: Center for Applied Linguistics, 1969), p. 100.

therefore, to maintain that one language or dialect is intrinsically inferior (or superior) to another is wrong. Black English is as good as standard English or French or Chinese and so on. The bias involved in considering one language inherently better or worse than another in communicating ideas can be seen, for example, in the ethnocentric position of Müller, a German, who in the *History of Ancient Sanskrit Literature* (1859) maintained that languages can be hierarchically ordered by their ability to conceptualize, with German (of course) as the "best" language.

The question of whether Black English Vernacular is deficient in its ability to express abstractions is perhaps best answered by the following brief excerpt from a tape-recorded conversation with fifteen-year-old Larry H., a member of a Harlem gang. The question raised for discussion is a metaphysical one. The interviewer asks Larry: "What happens to you after you die?" Larry responds: "Your spirit—soon as you die, your spirit leaves you. . . . Don't nobody know it's really a God. . . . You ain't goin' to no heaven, 'cause it ain't no heaven for you to go to."[35] These ideas may be translated as follows: "As soon as you die, your spirit leaves you. . . . Nobody really knows if God exists. . . . You're not going to heaven because there is no heaven." Since the languages are translatable in their ideas and concepts, it is obvious that one is not inferior or superior to the other in its ability to express abstractions.

AESTHETIC DIMENSIONS OF THE VERBAL STYLE

Even though no language or dialect can be said to be inferior or superior to another in its inherent ability to communicate meaning or express ideas, there is an aesthetic dimension to languages, where evaluations are relevant. This is the dimension of taste, value, style, and sensibility. On aesthetic grounds, then, it is perfectly legitimate to admire the superior lyrical quality of Italian, the "vitamins" of Yiddish—"Yiddish," says Isaac Bashevis Singer, "contains vitamins that other languages don't have"[36]—the precision of Ger-

35. Baratz and Baratz, op. cit.
36. Morton Reichek, "Storyteller," *The New York Times Magazine*, March 23, 1975, p. 8.

man, the flexibility and explicitness of standard English, and the "soul" of Black English Vernacular.

The best way to judge Black English verbal style is to listen. For Black English is mostly an oral rather than a written language. The ear is the best judge, also, since it is difficult in writing to convey the rhythmic complexity, tonal range, and tremendous energy of Black English. The style—dynamic, elegant, complex, and subtle—is often lost on the printed page. But some Black writers, especially those poets who use the vernacular of the people, *do* attempt to convey these stylistic aspects. It should be clear, though, that these writers are neither deprived nor lacking in standard English skills. Instead, they are still in touch with their primary native dialect, which they use as a symbol of social cohesion and unique cultural heritage. As Stephen Henderson notes, "Poets use Black speech forms consciously because they know that Black people—the mass of us—do not talk like white people."[37]

But to get a good idea of Black English verbal style listen to the children at play, to the recordings of the poets, to the Sunday preachers on the radio, to the disc jockeys on jazz and soul radio stations, and to the lyrics and voices of Black musicians:

> . . . the song stylings and instrumentations of John Coltrane, Pharaoh Sanders, James Brown, Aretha Franklin, Wilson Pickett, Sam Cooke, Sun Ra, Cecil Taylor, Ray Charles, *et al*. This is the essential energy that is Blackness, the lyricism of its consciousness. The *beat* as opposed to anything melodic. These voices, sounds, this mysticism: a kind of underground creative mixed-media biography. . . . From it we have automatically invented a new means of seeing. We have given a clarity, a freshness to English: a new turn, a vivid life. Our language is born of sound clusters, as opposed to Shakespeare's, which derives from the nexus, *sight*.[38]

Black English verbal style takes pleasure in wordplay—for example, rhyming and virtuoso naming and enumerating, which

---

37. Stephen Henderson, *Understanding the New Black Poetry: Black Speech and Black Music as Poetic References* (New York: William Morrow & Co., Inc., 1973), pp. 44–45.

38. Clarence Major, "From the Editors Preface to *The New Black Poetry,*" in *Black American Literature: 1760–Present,* ed. R. Miller (Beverly Hills, Cal.: Glencoe Press, 1971), p. 739.

are rooted in folk practices of nicknaming. In this regard, Henderson quotes a Black man in his fifties who defined "soul" as: "I don't want nothin' old but some gold; I don't want nothin' Black but a Cadillac."[39]

Delight in wordplay is also seen in the folk games that children play on the streets. "One of the more interesting is called *jonin'* by the Washington community—*sounding* or *the dozens* elsewhere." It is a quasi-ritualized game of verbal insult, with recognized rules for excelling and status reward.[40] When Dillard recorded these games, one of the more popular ones was verbal play based on " 'What did James Brown say when . . . ?' with an answer expected in the shape of a title from one of the rock and roll star's songs. Some of the youngsters showed an amazing inventiveness within such frameworks."[41]

A delightful example of the blunt style of wordplay comes from Ralph Ellison's *Invisible Man*. A street cleaner talking with Ellison's hero says, "All it takes in this here man's town is a little shit, grit and mother-wit. And man, I was bawn with all three."[42] Black English verbal style has a rich access to feelings and imagery that is often lost in more word-bound styles.

Finally, a word of warning. In every national group there is a form of the language that is designated as inferior and used as a means for discriminating against the speakers of that form. This exists in Britain, France, Germany, and elsewhere. Black English is the American version of this inferior language form. In this connection, Karyn Taylor warns:

> If white America listens to her newly tolerant academicians and believes that Black English is not "bad" English but rather a different language, valid and worthy in its own right, she might stop ridiculing Blacks for speaking their language. But she might also use this as a convenient excuse to further reinforce the wall of educational segregation and discrimination, thereby continuing to limit opportunity for Black advancement. What will happen if educators decide not to teach Standard English to Black English-speaking students on the grounds that their own language is a valid one yet continue to hold fluency in standard English as a de facto criterion for employment in higher job levels or entrance into college or graduate school?

39. Henderson. op. cit., p. 38.
40. Dillard, op. cit., p. 261.
41. Ibid.
42. Henderson, op. cit., p. 40.

... might not linguistic and cultural identity be just another way to effect the same discrimination and prejudice without having to call it "racism"? These are not reasons for Black America to relinquish her linguistic and cultural heritage, but they are possibilities to keep in mind. . . . the more firmly Black people assert their cultural identity as being separate and alienated from white culture, the greater the possibility that it can be used against them.[43]

IMPLICATIONS FOR EDUCATORS

Perhaps one of the most serious consequences of the "non-verbal" hypothesis is that it leads to erroneous compensatory educational strategies. Many of the compensatory programs of the sixties were based on the presumption of verbal and cognitive deficits for which corrections had to be made. This compensatory approach is bound to fail since it is rooted in a misconceived notion of "filling a vacuum"—a vacuum of linguistic-cognitive impoverishment that has no basis in fact.

The "verbal difference" hypothesis maintains that there are important differences in the language and learning styles of (and among) various inner-city groups. Although the difference often does present a problem to the child who is attempting to learn the language of the school, this educational disadvantage usually results from our failure as educators to understand the child's distinct language and learning style. But the verbal difference is also an important source of strength, and if the positives in the child's style are understood and used in our teaching, then the educational disadvantage may well evaporate. In this connection Ralph Ellison makes two important points: (1) human beings cling to the language that makes it possible for them to control chaos and to survive in the situations in which they find themselves; (2) the way to teach new forms or varieties or patterns of language is not to attempt to eliminate the old forms but to build upon them while at the same time valuing them in a way that is consonant with the desire for dignity that lies in each of us.[44] Thus, if we deny or take away the student's

43. Taylor, op. cit., p. 273.
44. Ralph Ellison, quoted in T. J. Creswell, "The Twenty Billion Dollar Misunderstanding," in *Social Dialects and Language Learning,* ed. R. Shuy (Champaign, Ill., National Council of Teachers of English, 1964), p. 87.

language, we deny and diminish a crucial aspect of the student who uses it.

In the "verbal difference" educational process, the children learn that their own language is not only perfectly acceptable, but that it is also the most appropriate language in the right situation—home, the handball court, and so on. But the children also learn that in more formal circumstances, for jobs and college, using the language of the mainstream culture can get better results.

The educational strategy based on the strengths of the communicative style presupposes that teachers have some familiarity with the languages and verbal styles of the students they are teaching, although of course they are not expected to be experts in nor speakers of Black English. Instruction in standard English for Black students should incorporate methods of teaching standard English while preserving the strengths of the students' primary linguistic and cultural heritage, as is done in bilingual education.

The specific issue of whether and how much Black English Vernacular should be used in instruction—whether, for example, Black English primers should be used in teaching reading —is currently an open research question and a controversial issue. Many Black parents and some Black leaders fear that using Black English in instruction might mean that their children will not learn "proper" English, and they understandably insist that their children have the means to make it in mainstream society. However, the educational strategy based on the linguistic insight of a distinct Black English language demands the same thing—that Black English Vernacular not replace standard English in instruction, but instead that the primary language the child possesses be understood as a *contact point* to the standard English of school. The essential point is not whether Black English is used in instruction, but rather that the teacher recognizes and understands the positive qualities of the verbal style of inner-city youngsters.

Knowing the language and the positive qualities of the child's verbal repertoire helps to establish contact with the child by accepting his or her *own* language, and sets the stage for an expectation of successful learning, since the methods are based on the strengths of the child. Specific educational techniques follow from the assets of the inner-city child: the highly verbal culture, the rich oral tradition, the skills found in street games, and the sensitive and integrated mode of verbal and nonverbal communication. Verbal and nonverbal games can be incorporated into language instruction to make learning congruent with the style of the child and also fun: role playing, dialect games, verbal games modeled on television shows such as *Password,* charades, puppetry, and so on. Frank Riessman and John Dawkins have developed a "Hiptionary," which in a systematic and formal way uses the hip vocabulary of the street vernacular as an entrée to learning standard English.[45] Learning while doing and while getting physically involved, based on an integrated nonverbal and verbal communicative skill, can be accomplished in many ways: learning about balance, for example, while building a block tower, or learning about local politics and history while taping interviews with leaders in the community and with grandparents, etc. Learning based on knowledge of the strengths of the child's distinct style is also learning based on issues of direct concern to the child: talking, reading, or writing about topics like "Why do I live in the slums?" rather than "Farm Animals," and so on.

There are many strengths in the verbal repertoire of the poor. The educational issue is how best to build on the student's assets while at the same time encouraging facility with the language of the mainstream culture. The educational emphasis, then, is not remedial, based on painful remedies for presumed failures, but instead supplementary, based on the positive qualities of the child's own language and verbal style.

45. Frank Riessman and John Dawkins, *Play it Cool* (Chicago, Ill.: Follett Publishing Co., 1967), pp. 3–27.

3

The Strengths of the Black Culture

The curtain of social, psychological, and cultural invisibility that has surrounded the poor and the ethnic groups in America is being penetrated. In the early sixties, Michael Harrington,[1] among others, called attention to the hidden poverty in America. The invisibility of Black Americans is an early and continuous theme in Black literature.[2] Thanks to the civil rights movement of the 1960s and the short-lived war on poverty, Americans have become more aware of the pernicious effects of social and economic disadvantage and of the need for corrective action.

In the academic community this awareness has resulted in an outpouring of educational research, which one can assume is for the most part well-intentioned. Some of this research has been used in the formulation of programs designed to alleviate inequality. Despite the good intentions, however, much of it, like the majority of earlier research on minorities and the poor, continues to reflect a negative bias.

Most research on the so-called disadvantaged has been conducted through a prism of white-middle-class norms, which are themselves more ideal than real. Few attempts have been made

This chapter was written by Elinor Bowles, Research Associate of the New Human Services Institute of Queens College.

1. Michael Harrington, *The Other America: Poverty in the United States* (Baltimore, Md.: Penguin Books, Inc., 1962; 1971).

2. See writings by Langston Hughes, Richard Wright, Ralph Ellison, James Baldwin, John Williams, and Sterling Brown for examples.

to understand the culture and behavior of the economically and socially disadvantaged from the perspective of the people involved. As a consequence, much of the behavior of these groups is labeled "deviant" because it does not conform to the "norms." The concept of deviance is explained by Howard S. Beckers:

> Social groups create deviance by making the rules whose infraction constitutes deviance and by applying those rules to particular people and labeling them as outsiders. From this point of view, deviance is not a quality of the act the person commits, but rather a consequence of the application by others of rules and sanctions to an "offender." The deviant is one to whom that label has successfully been applied; deviant behavior is behavior that people so label.[3]

The deviant label as applied to the poor and minorities displays a failure to recognize that some behaviors that are appropriate for dealing with white-middle-class life are inappropriate and ineffective in coping with the realities of poverty and discrimination. It also indicates failure to acknowledge that much of accepted "normal" middle-class behavior produces intrapsychic and interpersonal difficulties. Because of the deviant label, many characteristics of the inner-city population that represent positive efforts to cope with a stressful environment have been labeled pathological. The equation of nonconformity and pathology results from inadequate knowledge of the cultural patterns and coping strategies of minorities and the poor.

The purpose of this chapter is to pinpoint some of the cultural strengths of the Black community. The focus is on Black culture for three basic reasons: first, Blacks are the largest ethnic minority group in the United States; second, Blacks comprise a disproportionate percentage of Americans living in poverty; and third, the Black community has been the subject of most of the research and writing done on disadvantaged economic and ethnic groups in America.[4]

While the total configuration of cultural patterns described

---

3. Howard S. Beckers, *The Outsiders* (New York: Free Press, 1963), p. 9.

4. By citing these strengths I am not denying the destructive effects of social inequities or ignoring the fact that some individuals have been overwhelmed by social conditions. It should be clear also that other inner-city groups, such as Chicanos and Puerto Ricans, have different cultures and cultural strengths.

may be specific to the Black community, the individual characteristics and coping strategies find universal expression. Moreover, the following observations by no means are considered
definitive. They serve merely to illustrate that Black culture
contains within it strengths that have enabled Blacks to survive
if not to overcome; and that these strengths represent attributes
and skills that can be utilized by educators to help children
achieve in school.

The basic strength of Black culture should be obvious. No
other group in America has survived against as many odds or
fought as long and consistently to gain access to the society. Nor
has any other group had to utilize so many different strategies
in its struggle for equal opportunities.

During this three-hundred year struggle, Blacks have used
slave rebellions, the underground railroad, self-help groups, appeals to white self-interest, calls for racial separation and cultural nationalism, demands for integration, attempts at coali-
tion with other racially and economically oppressed groups,
verbal agitation, litigation, legislation, and direct-action techniques such as boycotts, picketing, and sit-ins. The struggle has
been for emancipation, anti-lynching laws, voting rights, equal
education, desegregation of public facilities, elimination of employment and housing discrimination, community control, and
equity in political participation. The call for Black Power in the
mid-1960s set the stage for a coalescing of many of these strategies. It represented the ultimate disenchantment with appeals
to white conscience as well as the demand for a new Black
consciousness and total participation in American life.

Equally obvious is the impact of the heightened civil rights
struggle of the 1960s on other liberation efforts. It provided the
model as well as the vocabulary for a string of movements:
women's liberation, gay liberation, senior citizens liberation,
Chicano liberation, Native American liberation, Puerto Rican
liberation, and on and on. "Freedom Now!" became a universal
demand. President Lyndon B. Johnson told the country: "We
shall overcome!" And because Blacks were audacious enough to
proclaim that "Black Is Beautiful," other ethnic groups began
to assert increased pride in their heritage, and a new form of
cultural pluralism was begun.

Obvious, too, is the fact that Black creative vitality has had a strong impact on American popular culture—particularly during the past fifteen years. The music and dance, language and style of the sixties and seventies embody much that is Black. Black plays and performers dominated the Broadway award-giving ceremonies in 1975. Madison Avenue advertising found a new font of inspiration in Black language. And the life style of many young middle-class white Americans, disenchanted with materialism, social isolation, and emotional constriction, has in large part been based on their perception of the more open, emotionally honest life style of Blacks (as well as Native American and other nonwhite cultures).

FAMILY LIFE

Black Americans have developed two particularly strong institutions: the family and the church. Both have survived in a repressive environment and both are characterized by functionalism and flexibility. Together they provide a strong emotional support system in the Black community. Each bears detailed examination because of its importance to the Black culture.

The nature of the American family—its structure and functions—is undergoing critical reexamination by behavioral and social scientists as well as feminists and those white-middle-class Americans who are questioning the gender roles imposed by traditional views of the family.[5] Under close scrutiny is the still prevalent notion that the male-dominant nuclear family is the only viable family structure for a strong, healthy, and productive society. This model probably fits only a minority of American families (primarily upper-middle-income white ones).[6] Nonetheless, some social theorists believe that lack of conform-

5. See Arlene S. Skolnick and Jerome H. Skolnick, eds., *Family in Transition* (Boston: Little, Brown, 1972); Louise Kapp Howe, ed., *The Future of the Family* (New York: Simon & Schuster, 1972).
6. The model contains a regularly employed and occupationally mobile husband/father who is the sole or primary financial provider for his family and the ultimate authority in the home; a wife/mother whose main functions are to nurture her children, provide emotional support and sexual gratification for her husband, and manage household chores; and children who in their early years depend almost exclusively on their parents for physical and emotional security and socialization.

ity to this model produces psychological and social disturbance, which in turn is viewed as the root cause for the creation and perpetuation of poverty.

Thus we have the basis for the general charge that has been leveled against poor Black families: that at the heart of the so-called deterioration of the fabric of Black society is the deterioration and dysfunction of the Black family.[7] Critics of this thesis (and they are numerous) assert that far from being the root cause of the social problems of the Black community, the structure and functioning of Black families result largely from the continuous pressures upon them; and that despite these pressures, most Black families remain viable. To quote Martin Luther King, Jr.:

> For no other group in American life is the matter of family life more important than to the Negro. Our very survival is bound up in it. . . . no one in all history had to fight against so many physical and psychological horrors to have a family life.[8]

In *Black Families in White America*,[9] Andrew Billingsley traces the Black family from its African origins to its current status. He shows that throughout slavery, post-Reconstruction violence, Southern segregation, Northern prejudice and discrimination, continuous unemployment and underemployment, and unkept promises of expanded opportunities, the Black family has remained the primary source of nurture and support for its members, thereby fulfilling the major functions of the family as an institution. The meaningful question, therefore, is not "Is the Black family deteriorating?" but rather "How has the Black family managed to survive at all?" Joyce Ladner, in partial answer, comments:

> The adaptations which are necessary for the [Black] family to make if it is to survive allow for an alteration of the larger society's rules and, most importantly, the creation of an alternative

7. This thesis has been most explicitly stated in the controversial "Moynihan Report" (*The Negro Family: The Case for National Action*, Office of Policy Planning and Research, U.S. Department of Labor, March, 1965, p. 5).

8. Quoted in Joyce Ladner, *Tomorrow's Tomorrow: The Black Woman* (New York: Doubleday, 1971), p. 3. Quotation from address delivered at Abbott House, Westchester, New York, October 29, 1965.

9. Andrew Billingsley, *Black Families in White America* (Englewood Cliffs, N. J.: Prentice-Hall, 1968).

mode of action that is more functional for the particular circumstances.[10]

Contemporary students of the Black family point out that much research is needed, conducted within a realistic conceptual framework that does not impose the idealized construct of the independent, male-dominant nuclear family. Future research and discussion must look at Black families in terms of their unique social, economic, and political position in American society, their internal dynamics, and the variety and complexity of their structures and coping strategies. (Before proceeding with our discussion of Black families, we should remind ourselves that just as there is no such thing as *the* American family, so there is no single model that defines *the* Black family.)

At this point it is important to examine a currently popular conception. A specific charge leveled against Black families, particularly poor ones, is that they are matriarchal. While there is nothing intrinsically negative in the concept of a matriarchy, current use of the term by some social theorists is accusatory. The accusation maintains that because of its supposed matriarchal structure the Black family is dysfunctional, and the achievement motivation, particularly for males, is weak. As a consequence, according to this theory, a large percentage of Black families are poor.[11]

There are at least two basic flaws in this argument. The first is semantic: a misuse of the term "matriarchy." The second is cultural: a failure to comprehend the differences as well as the similarities between dominant American norms and roles and those of Black families.

As a descriptive label for the Black family, the word "matriarchy" is a misnomer. A matriarchal society is one "in which some, if not all, of the legal powers relating to the ordering and governing of the family-power over property, over inheritance, over marriage, over the house are lodged in women rather than men."[12] Clearly this is not the case with Black American families.

10. Ladner, op. cit., p. 33.
11. "Moynihan Report," op. cit.
12. Margaret Mead, *Male and Female* (New York: Morrow & Co., Inc., 1949), p. 301.

Another characteristic of a matriarchal society is that it "would accept matriarchy as natural, inevitable and desirable. Moreover, it would include male roles that are accepted and respected."[13] Neither Black men nor Black women desire or view as inevitable a dominant role for the female and a subordinate role for the male. Lewis and Jeffers, based on their study of primarily Black low-income families, report that "a major concern of the low-income wife or mother is the man's ability to 'take care of' or to 'be responsible for' his family financially."[14] Attitudes and aspirations of Black "street-corner" men in Washington, D.C., have been described by Elliot Liebow:

> [They want] to be publicly, legally married, to support a family and be the head of it, because this is what it is to be a man in our society, whether one lives in a room near the Carry-Out or in an elegant house in the suburbs.[15]

"Matriarchy"—like "deviant" and "pathological"—is a label that contains more than a small degree of cultural as well as sexist bias. Herzog and Lewis point out that one of the two basic assumptions reflected in the application of this label to Black families is that "in these families the woman is dominant."[16]

The strength of Black women has been the source of voluminous literary inspiration and had been referred to by practically all students of the Black family. Ladner has pointed out, however, that "All dominant people must necessarily be strong but all strong people are not necessarily dominant."[17] She further notes that "strength" is often mistaken for "dominance," particularly in reference to Black females. Ladner goes on to say that much of the difficulty social scientists have in describing the true role and character of Black women stems from the idealized passive role of women in American society.

13. Elizabeth Herzog and Hylan Lewis, "Children in Poor Families," *American Journal of Orthopsychiatry* 40, no. 3, (April 1970): 377.

14. Hylan Lewis and Camille Jeffers, "Poverty and the Behavior of Low Income Families" (Paper presented at the Annual Meeting of the American Orthopsychiatric Association, Chicago, March 19, 1964).

15. Elliot Liebow, *Tally's Corner* (Boston: Little, Brown, 1967) p. 215.

16. Herzog and Lewis, op. cit., p. 377.

17. Ladner, op. cit., p. 35.

Black women as a group, however, have never been allowed the luxury of a passive, dependent role. They have had to develop an independence and self-sufficiency that would enable them to support themselves as single women, since a large number of Black females never marry due to the excess of females over males, to supplement a husband's meager income, or to support a family when the husband is absent or unemployed.

Some of the additional psychological demands placed on Black women have been summarized by singer Lena Horne:

> I think Negro wives, no matter what their age or background or even their understanding of the problem, have to be terribly strong —much stronger than their white counterparts. They cannot relax, they cannot simply be loving wives waiting for the man of the house to come home. They have to be spiritual sponges, absorbing the racially inflicted hurts of their men. Yet at the same time they have to give him courage, to make him know that it is worth it to go on, to go back day after day to the humiliations and discouragement of trying to make it in a white man's world for the sake of their families. It's hard enough for a poor white man, but a hundred times harder for a Negro.[18]

Black women have had to be strong. That they are as strong as is often imputed, however, is highly unlikely. Ladner contends that the strength of the Black woman has taken on mythical proportions that impose the added burden of unrealistic expectations from the larger society.

According to Herzog and Lewis, the second basic assumption in the matriarchy thesis, that the woman's earning power is greater than the man's, reflects a cultural materialism that equates strength and dominance with earning power:

> The readiness to apply the matriarchal label may relate to the overriding value placed on money in our society. Because the [Black] woman is believed to have greater earning power than the [Black] male, it is assumed that she must be dominant.[19]

---

18. Quoted in Camille Jeffers, "Some Perspectives on Child Rearing Practices Among Urban Low Income Families" (Paper prepared for the Regional Training Institute, Project Enable, Miami, Florida, July 11, 1966), p. 19.
19. Herzog and Lewis, op. cit., p. 378.

However, in *Strengths of Black Families*, Robert B. Hill, who is in agreement with the position of Herzog and Lewis, points out that the assumption of greater earning power on the part of Black women is erroneous:

> Despite the frequent assertions about their greater job stability, black women are more likely than black men to be unemployed. Earnings data tell a similar story: just as the earnings of white women are significantly lower than the earnings of white men (even within similar occupational groupings), the earnings of black women are significantly lower than the earnings of black men. . . . In about 90 percent of black families with working wives, the earnings of the husband exceeded that of the wife.[20]

Because of discrimination in hiring and job mobility, Black families, to a much greater extent than white ones, are dependent on the earnings of both husband and wife (with one or both sometimes holding two jobs).[21] These same discriminatory practices, which result in high rates of Black male unemployment and underemployment, cause many men to despair of ever being able to adequately support their families. Rather than live with the loss of pride that accompanies not being able to fulfill a primary male role in our society—that of provider—these men choose to leave their families. As a result, many women are left as the sole source of family support.

Black females grow up with the realization that they probably will be employed most of their adult life; and Black parents, aware of the economic realities facing their children, prepare both sons and daughters for the role of wage earner. This similarity of socialization results in male-female relationships that, although not free from gender conflict, tend to be fundamentally egalitarian.[22]

Black men know that the maintenance of their families and the survival of their community require that their women be strong. Black women understand the economic limitations imposed on Black men and realize that they must be psychological

---

20. Robert B. Hill, *Strengths of Black Families* (New York: Emerson Hall, 1971), p. 13.

21. Ibid., p. 46. Hill notes that in Black families, two-thirds of the women work, compared to half of the wives in white families.

22. Ibid., pp. 18–20.

and economic helpmates. The efforts to deal with the psychological and financial burdens created by discrimination and prejudice place severe strains on the relationships between Black men and women. Nevertheless, in the Black community the strong woman is not a pariah, but is both accepted and respected.

The matriarchal concept as applied to the Black family places the responsibility for poverty on the family rather than on societal factors. This thesis has been a deterrent to meaningful studies of Black family life. It has also tended to obscure the fact that the majority of Black families are headed by a male who is the primary wage earner.[23] If the Black community were to accept the matriarchal thesis, and its assumption of strong women and weak men, one probable result would be to put males and females into adversary roles. This conflict would have a destructive impact on the Black community, for it would deflect attention and energy from the basic sociopolitical causes of poverty.

A crucial means of adaptation and survival for Black Americans has been the extended family.[24] Some scholars maintain that it has its roots in Africa, where the extended family was the basic form of economic, social, and religious organization.[25] While there is no consensus on this point, most students of Black American life agree that the extended family, with its close kinship ties, has been a primary strategy for coping with historical and contemporary forces.

The extended Black family network is not a monolithic model, but has various forms and functions. Broad distinctions can be made between the Southern rural Black extended family and the Northern urban one. Lenus Jack, Jr., also distinguishes the "micro" extended family from the "macro" one and from

23. Ibid., p. 56.

24. The extended family is by no means unique to Black Americans. It has been a primary means of adaptation and mobility for all poor and immigrant groups in America. However, its pervasiveness, form, and functions have been different for Black Americans, who have maintained various aspects of this model over a longer period of time (with the possible exception of affluent whites, who have utilized the extended family as a means for controlling wealth and power).

25. See Ladner, op. cit.; and Billingsley, op. cit.

the broader kin network.[26] Essentially, the extended family is a network of relationships among kin, as well as non-kin, comprising households of varying composition that interact to provide emotional and material support.[27]

In his study of a Black extended family network in New Orleans, Jack lists its principal characteristics as consanguinity, self-identification, identification with a central figure of respect, ownership and inheritance of real property, extensive contact, participation in ceremonial functions, and cooperation. Though Jack notes that the central figure is usually the mother or grandmother, he points out that she is not a matriarch. Her influence is not derived from dominance or power to command, but rather from the value of her experience and advice.[28]

Based on her study of second-generation welfare families in a Northern urban community, Carol B. Stack has described the extended Black family as "a cluster of kinsmen related chiefly through children but also through marriage and friendship, who align to provide domestic functions. This cluster, or domestic network, is diffused over several kin-based households, and fluctuations in individual household composition do not significantly affect cooperative arrangements."[29] The Northern urban extended family is usually less stable in composition than the Southern rural one, and is more likely to include non-kin.

The cooperative non-kin network comprised primarily of neighbors and found most often in Northern Black communi-

26. Lenus Jack, Jr., "Kinship and Residential Propinquity: A Study of the Black Extended Family in New Orleans" (Paper prepared for the Ninth International Congress of Anthropological and Ethnological Sciences, Chicago, August, 1973).

27. Such a network would include households consisting only of nuclear family members, households incorporating other kin, and households augmented by unrelated persons. These individual households are in some ways autonomous and in other ways interdependent. Over a span of time considerable fluctuations occur in the composition of individual households as well as in the composition of the domestic network. Also, extended family networks often include "fictive" or "fictitious" kin: trusted non-kinspeople often referred to by terms such as "play brother" and "play aunt."

28. Jack, op. cit., p. 10.

29. Carol B. Stack, "Sex Roles and Survival Strategies," in *Woman, Culture and Society*, eds. Michelle Zimbalist Rosaldo and Louise Lamphre (Stanford Cal.: Stanford University Press, 1974), p. 114.

ties may be an attenuation of the extended family. This type of
network is characterized by Hylan Lewis in his introduction to
Camille Jeffers's participant-observer study of Black families in
a public housing development in Washington, D.C.:

> Families in the housing project with the most inadequate incomes
> "appeared to have the most extensive communication networks in
> the project." They are adaptive networks, essential for survival.
> They facilitate the elementary exchange of small goods and ser-
> vices among people constantly caught with small lacks.[30]

As mentioned, the extended family provides a range of
benefits and supports for its members. One major function,
material assistance, is seen most clearly in the exchange of
goods and services. Stack describes these exchanges ("swap-
ping") in great detail, noting that in the Northern urban network they are the basis for reciprocal responsibilities and obli-
gations.[31] Often taking the form of bartering, these exchanges
include money, food, clothing (especially for children), and
household goods. Baby-sitting and child care and "taking in"
families and individuals in emergencies such as fire, illness,
hospitalization, or eviction are also part of these reciprocal exchanges. The high incidence of informal child adoption in the
Black community is an example of a more permanent form of
"taking in,"[32] as is the "augmented family,"[33] where unrelated
individuals often exert major influence in family dynamics and
organization.

Such exchanges are an adaptive strategy for dealing with
material lacks and the exclusion from broader social support
systems. As Elizabeth Herzog so aptly states: "If you don't have
a bank account and you don't have credit, then you'd better

30. Hylan Lewis, "Introduction" in *Living Poor*, Camille Jeffers (Ann
Arbor, Mich.: Ann Arbor Science Publishers, Inc., 1967), p. v.

31. Carol B. Stack, *All Our Kin: Strategies for Survival in a Black Community* (New York: Harper & Row, 1974), p. 28.

32. Hill, op. cit., pp. 6–7. Hill states: "Since formal adoption agencies have
historically not catered to non-whites, blacks had to develop their own network
for the informal adoption of children. This informal adoption network among
black families has functioned to tighten kinship bonds, since many black women
are reluctant to put their children up for adoption. When they are formally
placed, black children are more likely than white children to be adopted by
relatives."

33. Billingsley, op. cit., p. 21.

have good friends [and family] who will help you in time of trouble."[34] In addition to their pragmatic aspect, these exchanges represent a level of trust and concern, a recognition of mutual need and dependence, and a sense of cooperation.

The cooperation of the extended family has fostered economic and educational mobility. The pooling of resources has made it possible for many children to acquire a college education. In his description of sources of achievement in Black families, Andrew Billingsley places heavy emphasis on the vital role of the extended kin network. He also notes the importance of community members as role models, sources of encouragement, and interveners with the larger society.[35]

The extended family serves also as an emotional support system. Members of the domestic network offer comfort and guidance in times of crisis such as illness, death, or family breakup. Techniques for coping with the psychological stresses of poverty and discrimination are learned through example as well as through discussion, beginning in childhood.

Socialization of the young is an important function of the extended family. In *Tomorrow's Tomorrow,* Joyce Ladner comments:

> Although she [the preadolescent girl] spends more time with her nuclear family, it is often members of the extended family, including aunts and uncles, grandparents, cousins and others, who serve this vital function as well. . . . Grandmothers act as permanent babysitters while the actual parents are away working, and when the absence of parents is more permanent. . . . The influence of the extended family upon the socialization of the young Black girl is often very strong. Many children normally grow up in a three-generation household and they absorb the influence of grandmother and grandfather as well as mother and father.[36]

Interaction with a number of significant adults, in addition to providing diverse role models, enables children to develop a broad repertory of interpersonal sensitivities and skills. In

34. Elizabeth Herzog, *About the Poor: Some Facts and Some Fictions,* U.S. Department of Health, Education and Welfare, Social and Rehabilitation Service, Children's Bureau (Washington, D.C.: Government Printing Office, 1967), p. 12.

35. Billingsley, op. cit., pp. 97–121.

36. Ladner, op. cit., p. 50.

their day-to-day associations with grandparents, uncles, aunts, and cousins, children learn to interpret a wide range of verbal and nonverbal cues and to be sensitive to personality and tempermental differences. They are also given opportunities to express different aspects of their own personalities as they regularly interact with others who have different degrees of power and interest in them.

Extended family networks have fostered cohesiveness, stability, and achievement in the Black community. They have provided material, emotional, and spiritual support and have been an important mode of socialization. Although the extended family model of the rural South is decreasing,[37] variations of this model, comprised of both kin and non-kin, continue as important support systems.

The Black extended family has demonstrated functionalism and flexibility in its adaptation to changing social conditions, and probably has significant meaning for today's larger society.[38] Skolnick and Skolnick state that "the isolated nuclear family characteristic of industrial society may prove to be only an unstable, transitional stage of the family between two kinds of wider sociability—an early one built on kinship ties, and a later one, only now emerging, based on ties of common interest or community."[39]

The transition from childhood to adulthood is swift for most children of low-income families. As early as ages five and six, many assume major responsibilities in caring for themselves and younger siblings and in helping with household chores. In

37. Hill, op. cit., pp. 6, 42.
38. Many middle-income Americans, particularly the young, women, and the aged, are venting feelings of social and emotional isolation. These feelings often are expressed through encounter, sensitivity, and consciousness-raising groups. Perhaps the most obvious expression of the need for increased interaction, attachment, and support is the commune movement. In " 'Getting It All Together': Communes Past, Present, Future," Rosabeth Moss Kanter notes: ". . . what many communes today are seeking is to recreate their version of [the] extended family of the past, in their search for intense, intimate, participatory, meaningful, group-based ways of life. In the midst of an advanced technological society seen as isolating, meaningless, fragmented, and machine like, today's utopians wish to recreate a shared life together." (Howe, *The Future of the Family*, p. 77.)
39. Skolnick and Skolnick, op. cit., p. ix.

their preteens many make financial contributions to their families and act as parent surrogates. In their communities they are confronted by debilitating environmental conditions of which middle-income children, even with the advent of television, are only remotely aware. Speaking of the children of poor Black parents, Joyce Ladner has said:

> For the Black child, whose parents are unable to provide the constant "surveillance" that is expected by the larger society, the world takes on a strong form of realism. So much of one's survival depends, to some extent, on how independent he can be and how much he can fend for himself when necessary. Children in the community are taught to be strong and not to allow others to take them for granted.[40]

Learning to cope with prejudice and discrimination, in its overt as well as its subtle forms, is part of the early training of Black and other minority children, regardless of economic status. Even as preschoolers they begin to learn that much of what they will face in life—the quality of neighborhood they will live in, their housing and education, the type of employment they will find—is related to their color. They learn that frequently they will be prejudged merely on the basis of color. They discover that few minority group members are in positions of power. Despite the efforts of parents, they soon realize that to be white in America is easier than to be Black or Mexican or Puerto Rican or Native American:

> By what sends
> the white kids
> I ain't sent:
> I know I can't
> be President.
>
> What don't bug
> them white kids
> sure bugs me:
> We knows everybody
> ain't free!

40. Ladner, op. cit., p. 65.

What's written down
for white folks
ain't for us a-tall:
"Liberty And Justice—
Huh—For All."

Oop-pop-a-da!
Skee! Daddle-de-do!
Be-bop!

Salt' peanuts!

De-dop![41]

For many, the school experience serves primarily to reinforce this awareness.

Yet somehow, despite the handicaps of racism and poverty, most Black youngsters grow up to be self-supporting, self-respecting adults. The early confrontation with reality and the concomitant socialization for independence and responsibility develop capacities for self-reliance and assertion in these children. Members of low-income groups learn to navigate through the bureaucratic sea of governmental and private agencies that have been set up to serve them. They learn to use their wits to survive in the streets of their communities as well as in the broader society. They learn to evaluate and select among extremely limited alternative strategies to achieve minor and major goals.

Most important, perhaps, they develop resilience, the strength to recover from early lacks and repeated hardships. It is a resilience that comes from "paying your dues" and learning something about yourself and your environment in the process. It requires determination. The protracted civil rights struggle as well as the large numbers of low-income Black and other minority adults who have taken advantage of expanded educational opportunities and innovational programs, despite the poor quality and limited rewards of earlier education, are examples of this resilience.

The resilience of the Black community grows in part out of

41. Langston Hughes, "Children's Rhymes," from *Montage of a Dream Deferred* (New York: Harold Ober, 1951), p. 73.

what might be called "the philosophy of the cool."[42] "Be cool!" is an often-heard admonition.[43] "Coolness" requires the integration of cognitive and affective responses under pressure. It requires the ability to rapidly assess a stressful situation, to understand one's needs, and to organize one's emotions and behavior so as to achieve one's objective and at the same time maintain a sense of personal integrity. To be cool is to maintain control. It is not indifference, passivity, or being unaware. It is, instead, "patience and collectedness of mind."[44] Coolness is a balance of strong and often conflicting emotions. As Robert Farris Thompson states, "Perhaps one reason many American Negroes sing a sad song happy . . . is that it is cool to sweeten hurt; it is hot to concentrate on the pain."[45]

On the flip side of coolness, there is the capacity for direct expression of feelings. Blacks tend to place a premium on being "up front" with feelings, whether anger, joy, or sorrow. For example, Black people usually are not unnerved by expressions of ordinary anger, for in the socialization process they have not learned to equate anger with withdrawal of love. Anger is more likely to be viewed as a momentary state that can have any number of causes and is often an expression of caring.

The history of the Black family in America consists of a continued struggle to carve out family roles and structures that could withstand the assaults of slavery, segregation, discrimination, and poverty. Census statistics, which are the basis for most assessments of Black family life, indicate the damaging effects of these encounters. What the statistics fail to reveal, however, are the nature and pervasiveness of the destructive social and political influences on Black families in America. Nor do the statistics reveal the mechanisms that the Black culture has developed in its attempt to counteract their impact, and the sources of the strength that have enabled Blacks to maintain their struggle for a viable family life.

42. Robert Farris Thompson, "An Aesthetic of the Cool: West African Dance," *African Forum* 2, no. 2, (Fall 1966), p. 86.

43. Ibid., p. 86. "The last spoken words of Malcolm X were: 'Now brothers! Be cool, don't get excited.'" (*Time,* "Death and Transfiguration," March 5, 1965, p. 23).

44. Ibid., p. 86.

45. Ibid.

RELIGION

The black man's pilgrimage in America was made less onerous because of his religion. His religion was the organizing principle around which his life was structured. His church was his school, his forum, his political arena, his social club, his art gallery, his conservatory of music. It was lyceum and gymnasium as well as *sanctum sanctorum*. His religion was his fellowship with man, his audience with God. It was the peculiar sustaining force which gave him the strength to endure when endurance gave no promise, and the courage to be creative in the face of his own dehumanization.[46]

Leonard E. Barrett, in a view shared by W. E. B. DuBois and others, contends that although the African slave was forbidden to practice his native religions in America, it was the world view provided by these religions that informed his adoption and adaptation of Western religion. It is a world view that believes in the unity and interrelatedness of all things, animate and inanimate, physical, mental, and spiritual: "Thus the world is not just an abstraction; it is a force field with all things interacting."[47] This world view resists the compartmentalization and either/or thinking that separates body from mind, feelings from intellect, flesh from spirit.

While there may be some disagreement among scholars regarding the extent of African remnants in Black American religious beliefs and practices,[48] there is consensus regarding the cohesive role of the church. In "Stylin' Outta the Black Pulpit," Grace Holt Sims states: "If the primary function of the church was to develop a will to survive, its ancillary functions were aimed at making survival possible. It was through these

46. C. Eric Lincoln, "Foreword" in *Soul-Force: African Heritage in Afro-American Religion,* Leonard E. Barrett (New York: Doubleday, 1974), p. viii.

47. Leonard E. Barrett, *Soul-Force African Heritage in Afro-American Religion* (New York: Doubleday, 1974), pp. 17, 22.

48. Prominent among those who do not accept this view was E. Franklin Frazier, who believed that the African slave in America was so completely stripped of his heritage that there were no continuities between his African and American experiences. However, he does acknowledge that the slaves adapted Christian theology to their own psychological and social needs. (*The Negro Church in America,* New York: Schocken Books, 1964, pp. 11–12.)

secondary functions that the church became the matrix out of which black society was to be cohesive."[49]

The church was crucial to Black survival both psychologically and physically. For the slaves, religion made life endurable; it promised justice, a better life after death, which was seen as a "means of escape from the woes and weariness" of the slaves' harsh existence.[50] Through their spirituals and expressive worship services, the slaves could vent their fears and anger as well as feelings of joy and dreams of freedom.

The Black church, together with some white churches, was instrumental in bringing escaped slaves north to freedom, and many Black ministers were outspoken leaders in the abolition movement. In many communities, the Black minister was the only generally accepted liaison with the white community.

More recently, Black ministers have been active leaders in the heightened civil rights movement of the 1960s. Most prominent was the late Martin Luther King, Jr., whose leadership in the Birmingham, Alabama, bus boycott is credited with having stimulated the Black activism that followed. The pulpit has been the launching ground for many civic and political leaders, including the late congressman Adam Clayton Powell, Jr.

Many secular institutions in the Black community have grown out of the church:

> The Negro church has provided the pattern for the organization of mutual aid societies and insurance companies. It has provided the pattern of Negro fraternal organizations and Greek letter societies. It has provided the pattern of administration and control of the Negro schools so far as they have been under the control of Negroes.[51]

Several Black banks and insurance companies that were a direct outgrowth of church burial societies and church credit unions are listed among the major business organizations in the country. Of the approximately thirty private Black colleges that are members of the United Negro College Fund, roughly 90

49. Grace Holt Sims, "Stylin' Outta the Black Pulpit," in *Rappin' and Stylin' Out*, ed. Thomas Kochman (Chicago: University of Chicago Press, 1972), p. 190.

50. Frazier, op. cit., p. 82.

51. Ibid., pp. 14–15.

percent were originally chartered by Black churches or church-affiliated individuals and groups, beginning during the Reconstruction period between 1865 and 1870. These were the first institutions of higher education for Blacks and continue to educate approximately 65 percent of Black college students.

One of the most important religious movements in the Black community is the relatively young Nation of Islam (Black Muslims), which has built its membership through appeals to racial pride, racial separation, and economic self-help. Besides operating its own school system, it owns and operates large-scale farms, retail and wholesale outlets, and manufacturing concerns. The Nation of Islam actively seeks membership from the working class as well as from marginal and isolated members of the community, being especially active in penal institutions. Heavy emphasis is placed on family cohesion, moral behavior, abstinence from drugs and alcohol, adherence to traditional male and female roles, respect for women, education, and discipline. Admired by many nonmembers in the Black community, the Nation of Islam is regarded as a model of organization, administration, economic self-help, and spiritual and emotional support for its members.

The church has been a central institution in the lives of Black Americans. It was the original Black self-help institution; it has served as an economic and social catalyst, as banker, insurance company, psychiatrist, lawyer, social worker, and educator; it has provided a sense of community. A safe place for emotional release, the church was designed to help Blacks survive in a hostile environment and achieve some gratification of their social and psychological needs. Through participation in church activities many Blacks have acquired and developed organizational skills and leadership ability, for which there were no outlets in the larger community. Many top performers, such as singer Aretha Franklin, received their initial training and exposure in the church.

Today, the influence and centrality of the church is believed to be on the wane, particularly among the young. However, it continues to play an active role as the center of social and cultural life for many Black Americans. Robert B. Hill states that despite growing ambivalence toward the church, "churches with activist ministers are increasingly taking on secular activities, and collaborating with local community action organizations of varying ideologies."[52] Among the social services provided by Black churches are day care centers, senior citizens groups, nursing homes, credit unions, housing developments, and scholarships. While it may be true that the role of the church is diminishing, it is probably also true, as many Blacks believe, that "If you want to get something done in the Black community, go to the churches."

COMMUNICATION: TELLING IT LIKE IT IS

The Black communication style, as displayed in language, music, and dance, is both complex and direct and is rich in nuance and subtlety. The most obvious example of the vitality produced by the combination of complexity and directness is Black music—often called America's only indigenous art form. A joining of African rhythms and harmonies with European harmonies, Black music is a complex synthesis of polyrhythmic and countermelodic strains which produces a congruent whole. Primarily because of the intensity and dominance of the rhythms (the syncopation), the emotional content is immediate and clear, though replete with nuances and subtle shadings.

Growing out of jazz and its derivatives, current Black dances—now the popular dances of all young Americans—imitate the polyrhythmic nature of the music. The entire body is in motion—feet, hips, shoulders, arms, head—each doing its own thing yet in complete coordination. These dances represent a body language that is stylized but never ritualized, spontaneous but controlled.

A key feature of Black music and dance is improvisation, where each performer is free to express spontaneously feelings generated by the music and the interaction with the other performers. Among musicians this often results in a sensitive dialogue. While the dancers frequently seem not to be aware of one another, there is, again, a sensitive interplay between partners. The overall impact of both Black music and Black dance is a fusion of feelings and energy with restraint and control.

As noted earlier by Irving Taylor, Black Americans typi-

52. Hill, op. cit., p. 33.

cally communicate openly with their entire bodies and are not
"word-bound," that is, confined to words alone or to the formal
use of words. Body language is used generously to convey feelings and thoughts. A facial expression, a toss of the hips, the
head, a hand, and occasionally the entire body, often communicate more than any amount of words. Black folks literally "crack
up" physically when they laugh and make extensive use of body
contact in conversation. Casual observation of conversation
among Blacks reveals a freedom and ease of body movement
that suggest an acceptance of the body and its inherent sensual-
ity.

   Though not word-bound, Black Americans do take particular pleasure in the imaginative use of words. Words are appreciated for their poetry and power and are regarded as pos-
sessing a life force of their own.

   In his acceptance of the National Book Award for *All God's
Dangers: The Life of Nate Shaw*,[53] historian Theodore Rosengarten stated that Ned Cobb, his collaborator and the Black
cotton farmer who is the subject of the book, was a "man of
words" as distinct from a "man of letters." Although Cobb had
not mastered the formal use of standard English, he treasured
words and used them richly:

> My grandmother and other people that I knowed grew up in
> slavery time, they wasn't satisfied with their freedom. They felt
> like motherless children—they wasn't satisfied but they had to live
> under the impression that they were. Had to act in a way just as
> though everything was all right. But they would open up every
> once in a while and talk about slavery time—they didn't know
> nothin about no freedom then, didn't know what it was but they
> wanted it. And when they got it they knew that what they got
> wasn't what they wanted, it wasn't freedom, really. Had to do
> whatever the white man directed em to do, couldn't voice their
> heart's desire.[54]

   The creative word power of Blacks, as well as the inclina-
tion to "tell it like it is," is demonstrated by children at play, by
preachers in the pulpit, and through the lyrics of Black music
and the language of musicians, poets, and the people of the

   53. Theodore Rosengarten, *All God's Dangers: The Life of Nate Shaw*,
(New York: Alfred A. Knopf, 1974).
   54. Ibid., p. 8.

streets. Stephen Henderson, in his insightful analysis, says about the connotative complexity of Black language:

> Certain words and constructions seem to carry an inordinate emotional and psychological weight, so that whenever they are used they set all kinds of bells ringing, all kinds of synapses snapping, on all kinds of levels. . . .
>
> Let us take the word "roll," for example. Here are some instances of its use: "Rock and Roll," "Rollin' with My Baby," "I'm Rollin' Through an Unfriendly World," "Let the Good Times Roll," "He was sure rollin' today," "Roll 'em, Pete," "If you can roll your jelly like you roll your dough . . . ," "Let the church roll on," and so on. The meanings connote work, struggle, sexual congress, dancing, having a good time, and shooting dice. They cut across areas of experience usually thought of as separate, but they are not mutually exclusive. . . . The poetic potential of all this should be obvious.[55]

Numerous books have been written on Black vocabulary, which is spoken and understood, at least to some extent, by Blacks whatever their educational or social background. It has infused vitality into the language of mainstream America, as we are reminded when Henry Fonda tells us in a television commercial, "What you see is what you get." About the impact of Black language, George Frazier, a white writer, has observed: "What nuances, what plays of light and shade, what little sharpnesses [American] speech has are almost all of them out of the Black world."[56]

Black communication is characterized by forthrightness, free expression of feelings, nuance, individualization, and sensitive interaction among participants. The blend of subtlety and directness produces an invigorating tension, a tension that underlies much of Black culture.

CONCLUSION

There is much important information that sensitive research can uncover about Black culture. However, very little truth is found in existing research, most of which contains a

55. Stephen Henderson, *Understanding the New Black Poetry* (New York: William Morrow & Co., Inc., 1973), p. 44.
56. Quoted by Hoyt Fuller, "Towards a Black Aesthetic," in *The Black Aesthetic,* ed. Addison Gayle, Jr. (New York: Doubleday, 1971), p. 10.

negative bias toward deviance and pathology in studying Black culture and provides answers based on theories derived without reference to the Black experience. To recognize and understand the culture and its strengths, one must read Black History and folklore, listen to Black music, read Black novels and poetry, and observe and listen to Black people in everyday life. Above all, one must beware of simplistic answers to complicated questions.

This chapter was not intended as a comprehensive account of Black culture. Its purpose is to give an indication of the strengths that have been the bedrock of Black survival. Some of these strengths that we have identified are: a world view that unifies life yet does not deny its complexity, the central role of the church and the family, a realistic approach to life, communication patterns that are both complex and direct, personal values based on flexibility and resilience, and sustained hope and perseverance in the struggle to overcome continued social and economic oppression. This is not an exhaustive list nor are these strengths peculiar to Blacks or minorities or the poor. But they do give an indication of the richness inherent in inner-city cultures that can be used to foster school achievement, personal growth, and economic mobility.

Much of what has been discussed regarding the strengths of Black culture is probably what is often referred to as "soul," a much used but rarely defined quality. Soul can perhaps be defined as being "into" life, experiencing life honestly and intensely, and reflecting these qualities in one's mood and behavior. Although often communicated in the midst of pain and suffering, soul represents a personal harmony that coexists with an awareness of internal and external contradictions. It is an individualized, creative approach to life. It is the determination to "keep on keepin' on."

4

The Hidden IQ

Intelligence tests measure how quickly people can solve relatively unimportant problems making as few errors as possible, rather than measuring how people grapple with relatively important problems, making as many productive errors as necessary with time no factor.[1]

Some years ago, a birthday party for a member of the staff at a well-known psychological clinic played a novel role in the test performance of a Black child. Prior to the party this boy, whom we shall call James, had been described on the psychological record as "sullen, surly, slow, unresponsive, apathetic, unimaginative, lacking in inner life." This description was based on his behavior in the clinic interviews and on his performance on a number of psychological measures, including an intelligence test and a personality test. His was not an unusual record; many deprived children are similarly portrayed.

On the day of the birthday party, James was seated in an adjoining room waiting to go into the clinician's office. It was just after the lunch hour and James had the first afternoon appointment. At the conclusion of the lunch break on this particular day, the staff presented a surprise birthday cake to one of the clinicians, who was Black. The beautifully decorated cake was brought in and handed to the clinician by James's clinician, who was white, as were all the other members of the staff. The Black clinician was deeply moved by the cake—and the entire

1. Irving Taylor, 1961, personal communication.

surprise. In a moment of great feeling, she warmly embraced the giver of the cake. James inadvertently perceived all this from his vantage point in the outer office. That afternoon he showed amazing alacrity in taking the tests and responding in the interview. He was no longer sullen and dull. On the contrary, he seemed alive and enthusiastic, and he answered questions readily. His psychologist was astonished at the change and in the course of the next few weeks repeated with James the tests on which he had done so poorly. James now showed marked improvement, and the psychologist quickly revised not only James's test appraisal on his clinical record card, but her general personality description of him as well.

The high point of this new, positive relationship came some months later when James confided to the psychologist that she had gotten off on the wrong foot with him on the first day in the first three minutes of contact. The psychologist was taken aback and said, "What do you mean? I was very friendly; I told you my name and asked you yours." He responded, "Yeh, and I said James Watson and right away you called me Jimmy and you bin callin' me Jimmy ever since. My name is James, 'cept to my very good friends maybe. Even my mother calls me James." Then he went on to tell her how he had changed his opinion of her on the day of the birthday party because of the close relationship he had seen between her and the Black psychologist.

This little story illustrates a number of things. First, it shows that the test is a social situation. The testing situation, whether it be a psychological test or any other kind of test for that matter, reflects a relationship between people, a relationship that is often remarkably subtle. And when anything hampers this relationship, the result is likely to show in the test score itself. This can occur on an individual test as well as a group test, an IQ test as well as a personality test, a subject-matter examination as well as a psychological measure.

The story also shows how the behavior evidenced in the clinical situation tends to be seen by the psychologist as indicative of the basic personality of the child. This is frequently done with little awareness of how much this behavior is a product of the particular relationship between the psychologist and the child, and of the testing situation as such. Children from different cultural backgrounds respond very differently to clinical situations and to the idea of being tested or evaluated.

The anecdote also points up the fact that a well-meaning, clinically trained, unprejudiced psychologist can have poor rapport with an inner-city child, not because of deficient psychological technique, but because of limited knowledge about certain cultural attitudes. In this case, the attitude in question is the feeling held by many Black people that the informality intended by nicknames signifies a lack of respect when it takes place across cultural lines. This does not suggest that the child himself was aware of this reasoning, but rather that he was simply reflecting his mother's wish that he be called by his full name.

The story of James demonstrates the importance of having Black psychologists and mental health workers on the staff of a clinic. The Black child need not himself have a Black clinician, but the presence of a Black clinician in the clinic can be indirectly influential. And finally, the story neatly illustrates the fact that scores on tests are not fixed and can be reversed dramatically when the relationship to the tester is improved. There is apparently a hidden IQ and a hidden personality that are often not revealed by the test and the clinical interview. In our story, James's IQ score rose considerably in the retesting and his personality began to appear in a totally new light.

Currently there is considerable questioning of some of the basic assumptions of the IQ test. Consistent with the incident we have just reported, the old notion that the IQ is relatively stable or constant is under heavy fire. There is increasing recognition that IQ scores of inner-city children do not reflect their ability, because the test items include words that are not in the experience repertoire of these children. But there are many other assumptions involved in IQ testing that have not been as fully questioned, and perhaps it would be a good idea to trace briefly the history of the IQ controversy.

At first the issue revolved around whether the lower IQ of inner-city children was a result of heredity or environment. Research indicated that environmental factors were apparently decisive in producing the higher middle-class IQ. Then Allison Davis questioned the applicability of the IQ tests to non-middle-class groups.² He wondered if the tests might not be impregnated with middle-class problems and language, and thus not be fair to inner-city youngsters.

What Davis did was to take various intelligence-test problems on which deprived children did poorly, and reword them in terms equally familiar to all children. For example, instead of "Cub is to bear as gosling is to 1 ( ) fox, 2 ( ) grouse, 3 ( ) goose, 4 ( ) rabbit, 5 ( ) duck," he substituted, "Puppy goes with dog like kitten goes with 1 ( ) fox, 2 ( ) goose, 3 ( ) cat, 4 ( ) rabbit, 5 ( ) duck." The required understanding of the relationship of the concepts is not altered by the revised form. If the child does not know the word "gosling," he can never demonstrate his grasp of the relationship required in this question. In other words, until the change was made, this item was functioning as a vocabulary test for the inner-city child.³ The reformulation changed not only the vocabulary involved, but also the structure of the sentence to read "Puppy goes with dog like kitten goes with ———." "Goes with" is substituted for "is to." This made the problem more understandable to inner-city children. Surprisingly enough, however, even though Davis's changes produced a test that was more attuned to them, inner-city youngsters did not improve markedly. Something else apparently was deterring them. It remained for Ernest Haggard to clear up the mystery.⁴

THE BIG THREE: PRACTICE, MOTIVATION, RAPPORT

Haggard reasoned that although inner-city children may have taken many IQ tests, they really did not know how to take

2. Allison Davis, *Social-Class Influences Upon Learning* (Cambridge: Harvard University Press, 1948).

3. Robert Havighurst, one of Davis's colleagues, points out that items requiring knowledge of the following words may touch the experience of the middle-class child but not that of the deprived child: fireplace, chandelier, wallpaper, salad fork, dining room. Words which might be more familiar to deprived children, such as pump, coal stove, kerosene lamp, and rain barrel, rarely appear on intelligence tests. Kenneth Eells et al., *Intelligence and Cultural Differences* (Chicago: University of Chicago Press, 1951), p. 18.

4. Ernest A. Haggard, "Social Status and Intelligence," *Genetic Psychology Monographs* 49 (1954): 141–86; and personal communications from Dr. Haggard.

these tests properly; they lacked meaningful, directed practice. They also lacked motivation, and their relationship to the examiner was typically distant and beset by fears.

Haggard decided to control each of these factors. He gave both low-income and middle-class children three one-hour training periods in taking IQ tests. These practice periods included careful explanation of what was involved in each of the different types of problems found on the IQ tests. The explanations were given in words that were familiar to both groups. Haggard also offered special rewards for doing well, and he trained his examiners to be responsive to the inner-city children as well as to the middle-class youngsters, thus greatly enhancing the rapport.[5]

Under these conditions the IQs of the inner-city children improved sharply. This occurred with only three hours of practice.[6] And it occurred even on the old IQ tests with the middle-class-biased items. Apparently more important than the content of the test items was the attitude of the children toward the test situation and the examiner.

Haggard also showed that when test items were read aloud

5. In the area of motivation, it is clear that middle-class children are more motivated to do well on examinations of the IQ sort because of the general emphasis on success and competition in middle-class life. Even where an examination is not directly related to a reward or a threat, the middle-class child strives to perform well. Part of the difference in IQ scores of middle-class and deprived children is due to differences in strength of motivation to perform well on an examination rather than to differences in intelligence.

This point is indirectly verified in a study by Elizabeth Douvan. At first, an examination was given to both inner-city and middle-class youngsters without any indication of its importance, or of an offering of a meaningful reward for satisfactory work. The result was typical: the middle-class group showed far greater motivation than the inner-city group. Later, the test was repeated, but this time a reward was offered for successful work on the test. As a result, the motivation of the inner-city group increased much more than that of the middle-class group. Thus, when the test situation promised rewards that were direct, immediate, practical, and meaningful, inner-city children responded at a higher level than when such rewards were absent. But this is less true of middle-class youth, who are more often motivated to perform at close to their maximum level even while rewards are absent. See Elizabeth Douvan, "Social Status and Success Striving," *Journal of Abnormal and Social Psychology*, 11 (March 1956): pp. 219–23.

6. Haggard, op. cit., p. 5.

to the inner-city children while they followed in their test book-
lets, these children did much better.[7] Inner-city children generally are notoriously poor readers. Consequently, their typically
inadequate intelligence test performance is partly a result of
that difficulty rather than of limited intelligence.

It might be asked at this point, why all the fuss—if inner-
city children cannot read well, what difference does it make
whether we say they are less intelligent or deficient in reading? The answer is that it makes a huge difference because of
the contrasting implications of deficiencies in intelligence and
deficiencies in reading ability. Reading skill can be improved,
certainly in the child and to some degree even in the adult,
when motivation is present. On the other hand, the old assumption was that intelligence, although it is affected by experience and knowledge, is much less easily changed or improved. Perhaps not much can be done in schools to help
inner-city children if they suffer from low intelligence; but
this point of view is more harmful if the problem is poor reading.[8]

It is noteworthy that the middle-class youngsters improved
far less than the inner-city youngsters in the Haggard experiment. This is because they were already working nearer their
capacity, and the new environmental input—that is, the equali-

7. Ibid., p. 5.

8. It might be objected, of course, that in Haggard's investigation the
underprivileged youngsters improved more than the middle-class ones because
the latter had the higher IQ scores and thus could not improve upon them.
There are two answers to this objection, one of which is somewhat technical:
Haggard points out that through the use of a special statistical method (the
Johnson-Neyman technique), the effect of the higher IQ of the middle-class
children was held constant or removed. (Haggard, personal communication,
1961.)

Second, and less technically, the argument overlooks a fundamental assumption underlying most intelligence tests, namely, that the IQ is relatively
stable, and that it certainly cannot be raised easily. Haggard's study shows, on
the contrary, that in a period of five days that included only three one-hour
practice sessions, the IQ of large numbers of inner-city youngsters could be
significantly increased. What seems to be involved here is that if the individual
or group is not functioning with high motivation, or if efficient test-taking
techniques have not been developed, or if rapport with the examiner is not
good, the resulting performance can be readily improved.

zation of the test environment—did not lead to the expansion of the gap between the two groups; rather it led to a sharp reduction of the difference.

If motivated practice in only three hours can make such a difference in performance on the IQ test, one can only imagine what a difference a change in environment on a larger scale would mean in reducing traditional class and ethnic differences. Furthermore, one must question the importance of something that can be affected with so little effort.

THE IQ CONTROVERSY

Despite their enormous inadequacies, intelligence tests continue to provide the major basis for popular wisdom about education, employment opportunities, and the social class structure. In recent years, Arthur Jensen, first in his 1969 *Harvard Education Review* article and then in his books *Genetics and Education* (1972) and *Educability and Group Differences* (1973), Richard Herrnstein in his *Atlantic Monthly* article (1971) and then in *I.Q. in the Meritocracy* (1972), William Shockley in various articles and speeches,[9] and Christopher Jencks in *Inequality: A Reassessment of the Effects of Family and Schools in America* (1973) have all accepted the IQ scores as the basic measure of cognitive skill, and, except for Jencks, have relied upon these scores to argue the genetic inferiority of those who perform poorly on them. Jensen in particular has coupled this argument with the claim that the compensatory education programs of the 1960s have failed, primarily because of their failure to recognize the genetically determined limitations of the Black and poor people for whom they were designed.

In looking at the past twenty years of IQ test research and criticism, one must ask three broad questions: How modifiable is the IQ test score? What is the evidence from the twin studies

9. William Schockley, "Possible Transfer of Metallurgical and Astronomical Approaches to Problem of Environmental Versus Heredity," *Science* 154 (1966); "Negro I.Q. Deficit: Failure of a 'Malicious Coincidence' Model Warrants New Research Proposals," *Review of Education Research* 41 (1971); "Models, Mathematics, and the Moral Obligation to Diagnose the Origin of Negro I.Q. Deficits," *Review of Education Research* 41 (1971).

regarding heredity and intelligence? And what is measured by
the IQ tests and how important is it?

MODIFYING IQ SCORES

In addition to the Haggard experiment (which, incidentally, was reported over twenty years ago), a number of experiments have demonstrated quite conclusively that the IQ
test score is definitely modifiable. The IQ scores of many children vary as much as 15 points over the course of their school
years, and for one child in 10, it varies by more than 30
points. Jensen recognizes that "direct coaching" can increase
the IQ score by about 9 to 10 points[10] and in his *Harvard
Education Review* article, he notes IQ boosts of from 20
to 30 points and "in certain extreme cases as much as 60 to
70 points."[11]

One of the dimensions to be considered in examining
the factors that affect IQ test scores is the race of the examiner. A number of studies (H. G. Canady, D. O. Price, Ruth
Searles, T. F. Pettigrew, and a task force of the American
Psychological Association)[12] show that Black subjects performed better on a variety of tests when there was a Black
test-giver.

A small recent study adds further evidence for rejecting
the assertion made by the proponents of the hereditarian
argument that the race of the tester is of no consequence
in the test performance. Alternative forms of intelligence
tests were administered to Black and white high-school-age
males. Whites scored higher than Blacks under the manual
administration of the test. When an alternative form of the
same test was administered by computer, the scores of the
whites remained essentially the same. However, "Blacks

10. Arthur R. Jensen, *Educability and Group Differences* (New York:
Harper & Row, 1973), p. 127.
11. Arthur R. Jensen, "Environment, Heredity, and Intelligence," *Harvard Education Review,* Reprint Series No. 2 (1969), p. 73.
12. Cited by Peter Watson, "I.Q.: The Racial Gap," *Psychology Today* 6,
no. 4 (September 1972), pp. 48–52; APA Task Force on Employment Testing
of Minority Groups, "Job Testing and the Disadvantaged," *American Psychologist* 24, no. 14 (1969): 637–50.

improved their performance on the computerized test such that there was no discernible differences between the races." The authors of the study conclude that computerized testing may circumvent problems such as "potential bias upon the part of the tester, both conscious and subconscious, and anxiety [for the Blacks] that may be readily induced where tests are administered by persons representing more advantaged backgrounds."[13]

A key feature in the hereditarian argument (made particularly by Jensen) is the assertion that while lower-socioeconomic-status (SES) children do not differ from other children on nonconceptual tasks, they score significantly lower on the higher-order conceptual tasks, Level II (LII) tasks, as Jensen labels them. Although he cites Cronbach's work,[14] Jensen fails to acknowledge Cronbach's suggestion that "lower-class children could equal or overtake middle-class children if they were trained in the usefulness of conceptual analysis."[15] A test of Cronbach's suggestion has been carried out. "The results did not support [as Jensen contends] the presence of consistent, significant race differences in LII ability, when SES was adequately controlled."[16] In closing, the authors of the Cronbach-style test declared:

> a significantly high number of lower-class children, who might otherwise be identified as LII deficient on such tasks, are able to reach a middle-class level of functioning when trained. The findings support Cronbach's beliefs, and are in opposition to Jensen's theory that I.Q. differences are a function of genetic differences in conceptual ability.[17]

13. Douglas F. Johnson and William J. Michal, "Performance of Blacks and Whites in Computerized Versus Manual Testing Environments," *American Psychologist* 28, no. 8 (August 1973): 698.

14. L. Cronbach, "Heredity, Environmental and Educational Policy," *Harvard Education Review* 39 (1969): 338–47.

15. Philip J. Scrofani et al., "Conceptual Ability in Black and White Children of Different Social Classes: An Experimental Test of Jensen's Hypothesis," *American Journal of Orthopsychiatry* 43, no. 4 (July 1973): 542.

16. Ibid., p. 551.

17. Ibid., pp. 552f.

IQ ASSUMPTIONS DISCRIMINATE AGAINST
THE INNER-CITY CHILD

Walter Murray has questioned the following assumptions which function either directly or indirectly to penalize the inner-city child.[18]

1. The IQ is measured by the use of brief exercises that have to be executed fairly quickly, while "many of the problems that individuals are expected to solve in real life require much time and concentration." The latter type of task is excluded from the IQ test. The brief exercises and the general accent on speed in particular work against many inner-city children. They take a long time to become involved in problems, and their potential may not easily be evidenced on short, speed-oriented tasks. They will, in all likelihood, show their ability only after they are absorbed in a problem. Many middle-class children have a similar work orientation, of course, and rural children find the speed emphasis equally distasteful.

Allison Davis notes that speed is affected by cultural attitudes concerning the importance or unimportance of speed, and by personality factors, such as "competitiveness, conscientiousness, compulsiveness, exhibitionism, and anxiety."[19] These personality characteristics are less frequently associated with the inner-city child's personality pattern.

2. The IQ score is based on the accuracy of the final answer to the IQ question, not the method of thinking involved in arriving at this answer. "In most tests the final score, or judgment of the student's intelligence, is based on the number of correct responses. Little or no attention is given to the method by which the student attacked the problem or the kinds of considerations he made use of in attempting to solve it."[20] In-

18. Walter Murray, personal communication, 1960.
19. Ibid.
20. Haggard reports the following: "In one study, children were asked to give the reasons for their answers to intelligence test items. In the case of one analogy item, 35 of the 60 children tested marked the 'correct' response, but not one of these children gave the 'correct' reason for marking it. The reasons given were on the basis of rhyming, synonym, etc., but not on the basis of making the analogy—the process which the test constructor assumed was being measured." Ernest A. Haggard, "Techniques for the Development of Unbiased

ner-city children do not possess, as one psychologist put it recently, "good avoidance conditioning for wrong answers." They
do not have a good sense for what is likely to be a poor answer
because they have limited test-taking skills. The teacher and
the psychologist are typically oriented toward getting the right
answer, and are less interested in the thinking processes involved, particularly when this thinking does not lead to the
correct result.[21]

3. Intelligence is assumed to develop and increase with age;
items which do not show an improvement with age are excluded from the IQ tests. The assumption that intelligence increases with age has an indirect effect on the measurement of
the IQ of the inner-city children. Characteristically, their measured IQ has been found to fall with age. Apparently, this is
because they have not been exposed to the experiences and
vocabulary presumed to be normal in the culture, and on which
all the IQ tests are based. If IQ exercises were not dependent
on these experiences, and instead measured skills that did not
improve with the age of the child, the inner-city child might
fare better.

4. It is assumed that intelligence is best demonstrated in a
school environment. IQ tests have tended to become tests of
scholastic aptitude. Intelligence may be relatively unimportant
in business, industry, agriculture, and so forth, but on the surface such an assumption does not appear to be very sound.

With regard to the highly academic character of the IQ
test, Ralph Tyler notes that

> so far as problem-solving exercises are concerned the typical intel-
> ligence tests lean heavily on academic, school-type problems,

---

Tests," *Proceedings of the 1952 Conference on Testing Problems* (Princeton:
Educational Testing Service, 1953), p. 3.

21. Haggard reports a study in which "the test constructor wrote out the
mental processes he thought were being measured by the items in his published
test. It was found that for some items over 50 per cent of the 152 nine- and
ten-year-old children gave logically defensible reasons for marking answers
considered 'incorrect' by the test constructor. Furthermore, whenever more
than one logically defensible answer to an item was given, the middle-class
children tended to give the 'correct' answer (in the opinion of the test constructor), whereas lower-class children tended to give the 'incorrect' answer (in the
opinion of the test constructor)." Ibid., p. 4.

whereas lower-class children frequently have had more experience than have middle-class children in dealing with the kinds of
practical problems encountered on the street and in the play-
ground. That is to say, it seems clear . . . that youngsters who do
not show up well on intelligence tests do possess abilities that
indicate some skill in solving practical problems and that suggest
potentialities for further education if the schools had broad
enough goals to utilize talents of these kinds.[22]

EARLY ENVIRONMENT AND THE
CHANGEABILITY OF THE IQ

Few people still maintain the old assumption that the IQ
is necessarily constant throughout life. There is too much evidence showing that it can be changed under varying conditions.
But an allied view has been advanced that is related to the
"constancy" assumption. This argument holds that the inner-
city child has been immersed in an early "impoverished" environment in which there is insufficient stimulation, thus producing a basic retardation, so that in effect his or her IQ remains
relatively low throughout life.[23]

One version of this argument maintains that the early environment of the inner-city child produces behavior similar to
that sometimes found in institutionalized children and in children brought up in isolation from society. At its extreme, this
view holds that the behavior of inner-city children is similar to
that found in the stimulus-deprivation experiments, where
volunteers are put in special respiratory tanks for twenty-four
hours. (Following these experiments, the subjects are unable to
concentrate, their IQ performance and problem-solving ability

22. Ralph W. Tyler, "Can Intelligence Tests Be Used to Predict Educability," in Kenneth Eells, et al., *Intelligence and Cultural Differences,* (Chicago:
University of Chicago Press, 1951), p. 43.

23. Donald Hebb makes the assumption that the early childhood period
is of decisive importance in determining later intelligence. He believes that
Black and poor white children have had insufficient stimulation in their early
development, and that this accounts for their lower functioning intelligence at
a later age. He accepts the intelligence-test performance as an accurate indicator of operating intelligence although he believes it to be a completely inaccu-
rate index of capacity—inherent intelligence. See Donald O. Hebb, *Organization of Behavior* (New York: John Wiley, 1949), chapter 2.

temporarily deteriorate, and they are somewhat confused in general.) The stimulus-deprivation thesis presumes that the inner-city child has suffered some similar lack of stimulation over a long period of time, particularly in his or her early life, and that this accounts for the child's low IQ. There are three levels at which this argument may be challenged.

In the first place, the stimulus-deprivation analogy seems extremely far-fetched because whatever one may say about the environment of those children, it certainly is not lacking in stimulation. Witness the crowded homes and streets, the parties, TV sets, sports, games, fights, and so forth. Second, the family life includes a good deal of sibling interaction, physical punishment, definite toilet training, and various responsibility demands. Regardless of the particular evaluation one may wish to place on these practices, they do appear to provide stimulation. This environment seems quite distinct from that of children reared in isolation from society. Finally, Haggard's findings further call into question the inference concerning "basic retardation," because if the IQ can be so markedly improved by only three hours of special training, surely the childhood experiences cannot have been so limiting or irreversible. It might also be added that much of the behavior of inner-city children in nonacademic spheres gives evidence of considerable spontaneity, a trait not ordinarily associated with a history of deficient stimulation.

WHAT DO IQ TESTS MEASURE?

Until now, we have not questioned the value of the IQ test itself. But is time to turn our attention to this matter. Although they do not argue that IQ is synonymous with educability, the hereditarians do use the IQ test as a predictor of educability. And there is every reason to do so. The makers of the intelligence test made "school progress . . . the criterion against which the value of the intelligence test would be judged.[24] For example, Lewis Terman, who introduced to the U.S. the standard IQ test, the Stanford-Binet, "restricted his choice [of test items] to

24. Jerome Kagan, "The I.Q. Puzzle: What Are We Measuring?" *Inequality in Education* 14 (July 1973): 6.

items from the school curriculum. . . ."[25] With measures of
achievement thus mixed into the composition of the test items,
it was no surprise to find a high correlation between school
achievement and what was labeled as genetically determined
intelligence. Indeed, those parts of the test that are most
achievement- and knowledge-oriented correlate most highly
with total IQ.

Whatever it is that the IQ tests measure, it is not self-
evident that these are qualities to be highly valued or sought.
IQ test results typically do not correlate well with creative
thinking.[26] Rather, as Erich Fromm pointed out[27] long ago, IQ
tests measure quick mental adaptability and might better be
termed "mental adjustment" tests. They typically measure an
individual's ability to do brief exercises in which he or she has
no intrinsic interest or involvement; they require speed and
rapid shifting. As we have already observed, many of the problems that individuals are expected to solve in real life require
much time, concentration and involvement, and this type of
task is excluded from IQ tests.

The IQ test is constructed so as to correlate highly with
traditional school subjects, and success in that special arena does
not necessarily correlate with aspects of life experience, particularly among the poor and the minorities. Developed to predict school success, IQ tests do their job relatively well. But
since the traditional school learning context is now recognized
to be desperately lacking in joy and opportunity, the validity of
a predictive measure based on the same restrictive and selec-
tive values that characterize the school should be examined in
a new light. Indeed, one might almost be moved to suggest that
lack of success on such tests might be a sign of superior qualities. In any case, there seems to be little if any reason to impute
inadequate heredity to those who perform poorly on IQ tests.

25. John Garcia, "I.Q.: The Conspiracy," *Psychology Today* no. 4 (September 1972): 42.
26. On the basis of a review of over thirty-eight studies, Wallach stated
that we may conclude that "intelligence test scores and grades on standard
academic matter are not effective signs as to who will manifest the strongest
creative attainments in nonacademic contests." Michael A. Wallach, *The Intel-
ligence-Creativity Distinction* (General Learning Press, 1971).
27. Erich Fromm, *Man for Himself* (New York: Henry Holt, 1947), p. 75.

THE TWIN DATA REVIEWED

A basic proposition in the IQ thesis put forth by Herrnstein, Jensen, and Shockley is that much of the intelligence (up to 80 percent) is determined on a hereditary basis. The three men argue, therefore, that disparities in intelligence cannot easily be reversed; that is, differences between poor and rich and Black and white will not be overcome by improving the environment of the have-nots. The hereditary argument greatly depends on four twin studies. These investigations attempt to show that identical twins reared apart in different environments have highly similar IQs because of their identical hereditary structure. Concomitantly, it is argued that the greater similarities of IQ scores among monozygotic (MZ or "identical") twins than among dizygotic (DZ or "fraternal") twins, when both are raised in the same environment, proves the genetic hypothesis.

Central to the studies of the MZ ("identical") twins reared apart, of course, is the nature of the differing environments. If the environments were not significantly different, then the relative power of environment and heredity would not be determinable. Leon Kamin, chairman of the psychology department at Princeton University, has shown that the studies of separated twins offer quite insufficient evidence for arguing the primacy of heredity. The most important of the twin studies—those by Sir Cyril Burt—turn out to be problematic in several ways, the most important of which is that the separation of the twins was never under experimental control so that degrees of environmental differences are not as purported.[28]

> Forty-one percent of the twin pairs grew up in homes that were highly similar socioeconomically; only 26 percent (12 twin pairs) were sent to families markedly different in social class. In nine of these 12 pairs, the twin who lived in the upper middle class home had a higher IQ than the twin adopted by the working class home.[29]

28. Leon Kamin, "Heredity, Intelligence, Politics, and Psychology," (Paper delivered at the annual meeting of the Eastern Psychological Association, Spring 1973).
29. Jerome Kagan, op. cit., p. 9.

In the second largest of the twin studies, that by Shields:

> In 27 cases, the two separated twins were reared in related
> branches of the parents' families; only in 13 cases were the twins
> reared in unrelated families. The twins reared in related families
> resembled one another more closely, to a statistically significant
> degree. That is scarcely evidence for an overwhelming genetic
> determination of I.Q. test scores.[30]

In sum, in 41 percent of Burt's studies and in 27 of 40 cases
in Shields's study, there was *no significant difference* between
the homes in which the separated twins were reared. Thus the
central experimental condition which had to be met to give
power to the studies, the differing environments in which the
separated twins were raised, was not met in half the pairs.
Furthermore, where the environments differed, the twin in the
home with higher income did better on IQ tests, lending support to an environmental rather than a hereditary explanation.
And comparing pairs of twins, those in more similar homes had
scores more alike than those in less similar homes, again lending
support to the environmental thesis, not the hereditary one.

Kamin further points out that Burt's data is dangerously
dependent on teachers' subjective assessments of pupils' intelligence.[31] And after citing numerous shifts in Burt's data from
paper to paper, Kamin concludes: "The numbers left behind by
Professor Burt are simply not worthy of serious scientific attention."[32] We must note further that the twin studies were per-

30. Kamin, op cit., p. 12.
31. Ibid.
32. Kamin, op cit., p. 11. Basic to the hereditarian argument is the finding
that the scores of MZ ("identical") twins reared together are more alike than
that of DZ ("fraternal") twins reared in the same environment. This, so the
argument goes, is due to the greater genetic similarity of the MZ twins. However, a study comparing ninety pairs of MZ twins and seventy-four pairs of DZ
twins found that MZ twins, especially females, were "more similar in behaviors
that are likely to be the results of similar experience, not heredity. For example,
identical twins were more likely than DZ twins to study and do their homework
together, to have the same set of very close friends, and to have similar food
preferences." The author concluded: "There is a difference in the overall environment of the two types of twins which will, in turn, influence the intrapair
differences. . . . It seems evident that the assumption of a common environment
for monozygotic and dizygotic twins is of doubtful validity. . . ." R. T. Smith,
cited in Kamin, p. 34.

formed only on white twins, and their applicability to other populations cannot be assumed.

THE DATA SUMMARIZED: A SYLLOGISM

If IQ test scores among Blacks and others can be raised through various devices including coaching, training, changing testers, changing the testing environment, rewording the language of the test, and most important of all, by a combination of these, then the immutability and power of the IQ test score is questionable.[33] If the twin studies are unreliable in terms of both the real difference in the environments of the separated MZ twins and the nature of environmental similarity of MZ and DZ twins raised in the same home, then the power of the hereditary argument is seriously in doubt. If IQ test scores correlate poorly with measures of creativity and correlate well only with school success because the test was designed to include measure of school achievement, then the importance and relevance of the IQ test is diminished.

If all the above statements hold true, then it would seem best to conclude that IQ test scores are far too variable and are affected by far too many factors for us to reach any conclusions based upon these scores; and the weaknesses of the data in the twin studies simply do not allow one to reach any firm conclusions about the heritability of intelligence.

PUBLIC POLICY CONSEQUENCES

It is not sufficient to respond to the hereditarian argument only from the point of view of the data, for the proponents argue for the public policy consequences of their findings. One

33. Many persons have made the point that the correlation between IQ test scores and social class reflects the fact that it is largely white, urban, middle-class persons, sharing a semantic network and common institutional privileges, who make up the tests. Deutsch uses the term "cognitive socialization" to describe the test-taking technique, the lower anxiety in the testing situation, and the greater capability of decoding the specific verbal and written instructions of the test that is displayed by white, urban, middle-class subjects. He observes that: "There is no reason to support that any of these factors is central to intellectual ability." Martin Deutsch, "Heredity Intelligence" (Paper delivered at the Social Policy Conference on IQ, New York City, May 1973).

must then look as well as the public policy issues involved.

The fact that this age-old hereditarian argument resonates at the present time is significant in itself. Its importance is very much related to the presumed failures of the sixties and the current backlash against social expenditures for the poor. This latter group of hereditarians, while presenting new evidence on IQ data, has reworked some of the well-known traditional experiments—experiments which are based upon very soft data, indeed—into their current hereditarian argument which is utilized to buttress a public policy that calls for the diminution of governmental aid for improved schooling for the poor and minorities. And not so incidentally this argument is also used to reinforce the notion that middle-class individuals are doing well in the world because of an innate intelligence that has led to their academic, societal, and economic progress. This is not a new function for the IQ tests. In the last fifty years, they have been used consistently to reinforce public policy directed toward limiting the opportunities of immigrants, Blacks, and Third World people. Indeed, in an earlier era these tests served to limit the opportunities of other groups, some of whose members today proclaim their infallibility.

Writing in 1917, Lewis Terman said, "if we would preserve our state for a class of people worthy to possess it, we must prevent, as far as possible, the propagation of mental degenerates . . . , the increasing spawn of degeneracy."[34] Reporting on a study he conducted for the U. S. Public Health Service based upon applying the new mental tests to European immigrants arriving on Ellis Island in 1912, Henry Goddard, another of the major importers of the IQ tests, found that 83 percent of Jews, 90 percent of Hungarians, 79 percent of Italians, and 87 percent of Russians were "feeble minded."[35] Five years later, Goddard was able to report that the use of mental tests "for the detection of feeble minded aliens" had vastly increased the number of aliens deported.[36] Of course, today it is the intelligence of Blacks that is in question. The early developers of mental testing had their say here, too. "[We] are incorporating the negro

34. L.M. Terman cited in Kamin, op. cit., p. 17.
35. H.H. Goddard, cited in Kamin, op. cit., pp. 24–26.
36. Ibid.

into our racial stock, while all of Europe is comparatively free from this taint . . . . The steps that should be taken must, of course, be dictated by science and not by political expediency. . . . The really important steps are those looking toward the prevention of the continued propagation of defective strains in the present population."[37]

Only William Shockley proposes restrictions upon reproduction. Jensen, echoed by Herrnstein appears more benign. Neither express support for limiting Black population. Rather, they are concerned with, in their belief, the effect of the false environmentalist argument upon Black psyches. Jensen notes that if Blacks came to believe their problems are caused by racial discrimination, past and present, it

> could generate a kind of racial paranoia, a belief that mysterious, hostile forces are operating to cause inequities in education and occupational performance, despite all apparent efforts to eliminate prejudice and discrimination—a fertile ground for the generation of frustrations, suspicions and hate.[38]

Besides expressing amazement at Jensen's belief in "all apparent efforts [being undertaken] to eliminate prejudice and discrimination," one must note that the statement is an almost classic illustration of what William Ryan has brilliantly labeled "blaming the victim."[39] Recognition by Blacks of the pervasive and continuing discrimination and prejudice in their lives is labeled paranoia, which Jensen argues could lead Blacks to behave in undesirable ways. Of course, for Blacks to accept the hereditarians' position that their fate is largely genetically determined is counsel to passivity, for what would be the sense of struggle if one's success in society is already predetermined and unmodifiable. Thus the public policy consequences of the hereditarians' argument are a reactionary's double delight—a cutback of "the massive expenditures [made on] misguided,

---

37. C. Brigham, cited in Kamin, op. cit., pp. 24–26. Discussing the author of this passage, Kamin notes, "With this contribution behind him, Brigham moved on to the secretaryship of the College Entrance Examination Board, where he devised and developed the Scholastic Aptitude Test; and at length to the Secretaryship of the American Psychological Association." Ibid.

38. Jensen, *Educability and Group Differences*, p. 21.

39. William Ryan, *Blaming the Victim* (New York: Pantheon, 1971).

irrelevant and ineffective remedies,"[40] and passive acceptance by Black people of their fate.

I look to a different strategy. I believe that little has been done to affect the environment to the extent appropriate to the magnitude of the problem, and what has been done has been misfocused on a "compensatory" formulation. And I see nothing in the very weak data of the hereditarians that is compelling. Thus, until we have tested fully the limits of the environmental approach, there is no reason to adopt the cynical and reactionary hereditarian dogma.

In the last analysis, the debate about the role of heredity and environment in relation to Black/white difference on IQ scores is both abstract and absurd. In the abstract, we certainly can agree that both heredity and environment affect IQ scores, creativity, intelligence, and cognitive functioning, as well as height, physical structure, and the like. But in the specific, the hereditary factors can only appear to the extent that the environment brings them out, so to speak. For example, there is no question that heredity and environment both affect differences in height between individuals and groups. So, in general, Swedes are taller than Japanese. But if the nutritional environment or any other environmental feature is available in only limited fashion to the Swedes, their hereditary tallness will not appear; they may be dwarfed in relation to the Japanese, assuming the latter have a fairly optimal environment with regard to nutrition, exercise, stimulation, sunlight, and a whole series of other environmental factors. Similarly, the hereditary cognitive potential of Blacks can only be shown if their environment for this particular characteristic is at least minimal, and preferably optimal. There is little question that the environmental preparation for IQ score functioning, whatever that may mean with regard to real intelligence, creativity, cognitive skill and the like, has clearly been deficient for large numbers of American Blacks. Hence, the hereditary potential with regard to this kind of functioning doesn't appear. As in the example of the deprived Swedes, American Blacks are functioning far beneath their hereditary potential.

In conclusion, it may be useful to quote from the remarks of Jerrold Zacharias, the physicist and educator:

40. Jensen, *Educability and Group Differences*, p. 21.

I will conclude by proposing that we not retreat to catch phrases like, I know these tests are not very good, but they are all we have. There are many other ways to assess a child's general competence. They may not look numerical or scientific, but they are known to every teacher and every school principal.

I believe, therefore, that the administration of IQ tests as they now exist should cease and desist. There should be a major effort to find some reasonable collection of procedures so that the need felt by teachers, school systems, and parents can be satisfied without at the same time destroying any children, teachers, school systems, or parents.[41]

41. Jerrold Zacharias, "The Trouble with I.Q. Tests," *Principal* 54, no. 4 (March/April 1975), p. 30. See this entire issue of *Principal* magazine for an extensive discussion of IQ tests.

5

Cognitive Style and How to Use It

In order to utilize the strengths of inner-city youngsters, it is necessary to understand their cognitive or learning styles. But first we must understand what is meant by cognitive style. Students of learning have focused a good deal on rather abstract and molecular concepts that have been derived from studies of pigeons and rats by B. F. Skinner and Clark L. Hull. These concepts of learning are useful, but what has been overlooked is the potential value of a more holistic, molar dimension of learning, which operates on the phenomenal level and which we refer to as "style."

One index of style relates to whether an individual learns things most easily by reading or hearing, or whether he or she learns by physically doing things. These examples are not to be conceived of as separate from one another; such combinations as a visual-physical learner are possible. Other dimensions of style reveal different aspects of learning custom. For example, some people like to work under pressure; they like a deadline and they like tests. Some people like to leave a lot of time for their work, enjoying a slow tempo. Some people like to work for long periods of time without a break; some like to work in a cold room, others in a warm one. Some people like to think while walking, some like to shift places and take frequent breaks. Some people take a long time to warm up, whereas others get into their work very quickly. Some people like to have all the facts in front of them before they can do any generalizing, and others prefer to have only a few facts. Typically, *people do not know their own style* nearly well enough.

COGNITION VERSUS EMOTION

Guidance counselors have focused far too much on the categories of emotion, motivation, and personality rather than on the cognitive categories of learning and thinking. There has been too much emphasis on the emotional approach in attempting to understand why a child doesn't learn. Little careful analysis is given to how the child's learning might improve simply by concentrating on the way that he or she works and learns, rather than on the affective reasons for not learning. Today if a child doesn't learn, it is quickly assumed that the difficulties must be due to some emotional block or conflict, or a learning disability. There is a different way of looking at the problem. Children may not be learning because their methods of learning are not suited to their style, and hence they cannot best utilize their mental power. Even where their troubles are in part emotional or due to inner conflict, it still may be possible to ignore this particular approach and concentrate profitably on the specific expression of the difficulty itself—the learning pattern.

If one rejects the premise that the emotional causes have been overemphasized, one may nevertheless give a willing ear to the possibility of dealing with crucial problems of learning in nonemotional, nonpsychodynamic terms. Unfortunately, teachers too often behave like psychologists and social workers. They do not sufficiently stress learning processes and styles of learning, apparently preferring motivational categories. One way to build appropriate prestige in the teaching profession is simply not to borrow from psychologists and sociologists, but to concentrate on the development of what education is most concerned with—teaching and learning.

Teacher-education courses in learning, educational psychology, and the like borrow heavily from animal-learning experiments. Such courses are victimized by the fact that the particular concepts and formulations developed in the animal literature are not easily applicable to human learning problems —for example, whether a child learns slowly, is a physical learner, is aural or visual, or whether it takes him or her a long time to warm up. When educational psychology courses have actually studied human learning, the focus has not been on the significant problems that are related to style. In attempting, for example, to deal with study habits, these courses are entirely too general. There is a great deal more to study habits than is explained in the usual introductory psychology textbook. The typical suggestions in these works are based upon various experiments which seem to indicate that distributive learning is the best approach, that one should survey material first, etc. But very little in these books addresses the idiosyncratic factors that are involved in learning.

For example, some people simply can't tolerate surveying a chapter before reading it. They become so anxious and disturbed by being asked to look at the overall view of the chapter that they can't function. These people want very much to read a chapter atomistically; this is their style. It won't help simply to tell such a person that he or she is not proceeding in the right way, and the same is true in terms of the general recommendation that one should have a quiet place to study. Strangely enough, at least to those who prefer quiet, some people study quite well in a noisy place, or with certain kinds of noise. Completely quiet places are not best for them. Some people take a long time to warm up; consequently, a great deal of spacing (or distribution) of learning would not be useful to them. This is their style. But the textbook does not tell you this because, in general, spaced or distributive learning has proved to be most effective.

The same argument applies to examinations or tests. For some people a test provides just the right mild anxiety to stimulate the integration of a great deal of material that must be learned. On the other hand, for large numbers of people tests are terrible because the tests disorganize them, make them too anxious, and thus prevent them from working. Tests are not conducive to the learning style of these individuals. When others argue that tests are marvelous because they aid pupils by providing corrections and criticism, they are referring to persons with a different style. Undoubtedly, tests work well for some pupils, but there are others who forget the corrections on tests because it disturbs them too much to remember their wrong answers.

There is a great deal of controversy in the traditional literature on the very question of whether repression of wrong answers occurs or whether "punishment" for giving wrong answers on tests helps to produce better recall. I am suggesting that two different styles are involved here. For some people the information that they gave wrong answers is extremely useful and challenging. If this information is called to their attention in a positive and stimulating way, it can be very constructive, making the wrong answer the figure in the foreground. But for other people, knowing that they have made a mistake is extremely disturbing and destructive of their morale, and it leads them to repress this material. Therefore, depending upon one's style and one's way of dealing with these problems, tests may or may not be useful.

STRATEGIES OF MODIFICATION

The task of the educator is to try to formulate the possible ways in which the strengths of the individual's learning style can be utilized and the weaknesses reduced or controlled. In approaching the problem, the first aim is to have the person become aware of the strengths and potentials in his or her style —because this is going to be the source of power. Thus, if an individual has a physical style, he or she has to learn the special attributes of this style and how to use them. The guidance counselor or teacher will have to help overcome the invidious interpretations of this style that are prevalent in our society. An example of a learning style that can be accommodated in the classroom is the "games" focus of some low-income youngsters. They like to learn things through games rather than through tests. An educator who devises a teaching method in the form of a game will have an excellent technique for winning the interest of these youngsters.

An inner-city youngster who likes to learn by listening and speaking—aural style—is unlikely to change completely and become, say, a reader. This is not to suggest that such pupils will not learn to read and write fluently, but their best learning, the long-lasting, deep learning that gets into their muscles, may derive from speaking and hearing.

Take an illustration of a different type. An inner-city youngster tells us that he sits down to work but cannot concentrate. It is extremely important at this point (and this is crucial in the diagnosis of style) to ascertain as precisely as possible exactly what takes place in this youngster's routine. For example, when does he study? What time does he come home from school? What does he do first when he comes into the house? Where does he study? He may say:

> I come home, throw down my books, and then I start to remember that I have to do some work. So I get out my books. I try to work. I take out the book, but my mind wanders. I look at the book; I look away. I can't get into the work, and after a few minutes of trying this, I begin to feel discouraged; I begin to feel bad. I feel I can't work. I'm no good. I get very worried, and then I run away from the work.

There are many possibilities operating in this pattern. One possibility is that this youngster has a slow warm-up period. He does not easily get into something new; he does not shift from whatever he has been doing before, whether he's been outside playing ball or inside listening to the radio. This may be due to a number of reasons. He may be a physical learner. If he is a physical learner, he must be involved physically in the work process. He has to get his muscles into it, and this takes time. If this is our student's pattern, then he must come to understand that although he is slow to warm up, this is not necessarily a negative quality; it is simply a different way of approaching work.

A student with a slow warm-up style may have a great deal of perseverance, once he gets involved. Once he is immersed, he may go deeper and deeper and not be able to shift away from the work easily. The inability to shift then doesn't operate as a negative feature, but as a positive element in his style. But the youngster described here rarely gets to this point. It's not that he doesn't persevere somewhere—for instance, in baseball or somewhere else. But in his school work he's never gotten past the point of the slow warm-up. He usually schedules his time so that he works for one hour. That's too little time because it takes him a half-hour to warm up. Even if he is successful and sticks with his work for the half-hour as a result of a teacher's or guidance worker's support and stimulation, he will have only a short time left to work at the end of the half-hour warm up. Consequently, this student has to plan a longer time period of work, recognizing in advance that it will take him about a half-hour to warm up. In other words, the person who would help him must give him a definition of his work pattern so that he may realize the positive potentialities in it.

When this new definition is provided, it is probable that a number of consequences will follow. Over a period of time the warm-up period will shorten, because part of the difficulty in the long warm-up is the anxiety that emerges. As an individual works, his anxiety decreases and, concomitantly, his interest has a chance to increase.

STRENGTH OVER WEAKNESS

Let us take another example, one in which the person's strengths can be used to deal with his weaknesses. How do you teach people how to read when reading is not their basic style? Everyone is going to need reading and writing ability regardless of his or her style. In order to teach reading to youngsters for whom it is stylistically uncongenial, one may want to use role playing, which is more related to the action style of the individual. The child can read about something that he or she has just acted out, or the youngster can read about a trip that was recently taken. While teaching reading under these conditions, teachers must remember that they are not developing a reading style; they are developing a skill, a balance in the pupil's style. The child is developing minimal efficiency in an area that is not rooted in his or her learning style. In a sense the teacher is going after the Achilles heel—the weakness, in this case the reading difficulty—by developing it through the child's strength, whether it be visual, aural, or physical. This is a basic tactic for defeating or limiting the weakness: connecting it and subjecting it to the strengths.

There are some other ways one can employ the strategy of style. Various transitional techniques can be used, for example, in overcoming some of a pupil's educational weaknesses. For example, inner-city youngsters ordinarily come to the school situation with a very poor auditory set. They are not accustomed to listening to people read stories to them. This kind of pattern can be overcome. Effective teachers can teach these children to learn through listening even though this may not be their best mode of learning. One technique is simply to make a game out of the auditory problem. The teacher asks, for example, "What is six and five?" Everybody in the class must answer several times. The pupil cannot fall asleep in such a class. Answering once doesn't leave the child free because he or she may be asked the same question or, perhaps different ones often. This is an excellent technique for waking up youngsters, and it has been effective with low-income students who customarily are not used to listening for extended periods of time. The objective of the game is to bring the children up to minimal listening ability. In areas of weakness our primary aim should be to establish functioning at a minimal level of adequacy so that weaknesses will not destroy strengths. Techniques of the kind described may be useful in reversing habits and sets that have grown out of the negative aspects of the person's style.

POOR OR SLOW?

An interesting confusion prevails in education circles between the "poor learner" and the "slow learner." The two are assumed to be identical. But need this be so? In a pragmatic culture such as ours, oriented toward quantity, speed, and measurement, this error is an easy one to make. In the classroom it is terribly easy to believe that the child who learns the lesson quickly is a better learner than one who takes a long period of time. But the problem is more complicated. The child who learns a subject more slowly is likely to be ignored and, unwittingly, discouraged by teachers. Even if they do not ignore the youngster but, on the contrary, give him or her special attention, they may reflect their implicit assumption that the child is a poor student. They may demand less of the child, for example. The point is that teachers never see the slowness as simply another style of learning with potential strengths of its own; nor do they see potential weaknesses in the fast learner, who may become glib or impatient with tasks requiring protracted attention. Because of the treatment they receive in the school system, slow learners may become poor learners.

It is time to put an end to the negative description of the term "slow" in the learning process. Slowness can reflect many things. It can indicate caution, a meticulous style, a desire to be very thorough, great interest which may constrain against rushing through a problem, or it may indicate a desire to mull things over. It may also indicate intellectual inadequacy. Extreme slowness probably does connote inadequacy in the absence of counterindications. Even here we have to be very careful to check all possible blocks, not only the obvious emotional disturbances. There may be many other types of blockage as well, such as auditory blocks, reading difficulties that are not of emotional origin, antagonism to the teacher, and so forth. The nature of the slowness itself also has to be carefully examined. A delayed result does not necessarily mean a slow process of thinking. Because children take a long time to arrive at an answer does not mean that their thinking is retarded. It may be that their thinking is more circuitous, that they are easily distracted, that they will not venture an answer until they are certain, and a host of other possibilities.

While our middle-class culture emphasizes speed, there is really no reason to assume that gifted, creative people have to learn or perform rapidly. We have to become accustomed to the idea of a slow gifted child. Some people take a long time to learn basic concepts, but when they finally do so, they may use these ideas in a thoughtful, penetrating fashion. Others may learn a concept rapidly and then switch to some other area without ever pursuing the original concept in depth. There are many slow people who demonstrate their intellectual power only on tasks that take them a long time to get interested in, and that have no time requirements. I have seen a fairly large number of college students whose grades and IQ scores were low, but who performed quite brilliantly on particular problems or in subjects in which they were deeply immersed. Their poor averages were simply a reflection of the pace required in college, a pace that was not attuned to their own style of work. They often failed courses where they could have done extremely well if given more time. Actually, an extended college program—say, five years—would benefit these students immeasurably. Educators tend to think of shortening college to three years for students who supposedly do not require the usual four years. But is there any reason why college could not be lengthened for students who have a different style and pace of work? Many of these youngsters do, in fact, attend college for

five or more years because they have to go to summer school
to make up the courses they fail when carrying a schedule that
is too heavy for them.

I had the opportunity of observing over a long period of
time a highly skilled mechanic who came from a low-income
background. Whenever he built anything in his house, such as
a table or a finished basement, he did so in a meticulous fashion;
it was the same when he worked on his car. He seemed to like
to work in this manner, mulling things over, taking his time.
Most old-time skilled workers like a leisurely pace. The shoe-
maker does not rush through his work, as a rule, but tends to
do it carefully, patiently, at a moderate clip. This often reflects
pride in the finished product. Apparently, then, in things that
are taken very seriously, things of deep concern such as matters
of personal pride, the slow style takes over.

DEVELOPING SELF-AWARENESS OF STYLE

Beth Atwood has developed some valuable classroom techniques for furthering students' awareness of their own and
other learning styles. She asks them to survey their own and
their classmates' ways of learning. The surveys include some of
the following items:

a. I am most alert for learning new things in the: (1) early morning,
(2) midday, (3) late afternoon or (4) evening.
b. The easiest way(s) for me to learn something is to: (1) read it, (2)
hear it, (3) see it in pictures, (4) try it, (5) write it in my own words,
(6) explain it to someone else or (7) draw a diagram or picture of
it.
c. The kinds of learning situations that bother me most are: (1)
large group sessions, (2) small group sessions, (3) using learning
games such as spelling bees, (4) working with a partner the teacher
chose for me, (5) working with a partner who chose me, (6) working with a partner I don't know, (7) working by myself, (8) working
on team projects, (9) working in a very quiet place, (10) working
in a very noisy place, (11) being interrupted while I'm working,
(12) having to take a break in the middle of my work, (13) having
to stop when I'm not finished or (14) having nothing to do while
I wait for others to finish.[1]

1. Beth S. Atwood, "Helping Students Recognize Their Own Learning
Styles," *Learning* 3, no. 2 (April 1975): 73–74.

Atwood also "encourages students to read about and collect examples of people who work in nonroutine fashions. This will help them recognize the diversity of learning styles that are possible and how these styles or patterns differ from one person to another. For example, artists, writers, and inventors are famous for working and studying at odd hours, sometimes needing absolute solitude or, at other times, wanting constant contact with people."[2]

COGNITIVE STYLE MAPPING

"Cognitive style mapping" is the term used to describe a process by which the individual is first assessed of his or her most comfortable manner of learning, whether it be visual or auditory, independent or in a group. One place where cognitive style mapping is currently practiced is Oakland Community College in Oakland, Michigan. When students seek admission to the school, they find among the more traditional entrance exams a few tests that ask them to taste cheese, listen to music, and assemble puzzles. These unusual activities are not intended as simple diversions, but are specifically designed to discover how the students perceive their world. The purpose of the tests is to help tailor the students' education to reflect the way they learn and thereby offer the greatest likelihood of success in learning.

One report on Oakland Community College's cognitive style mapping summarizes the program this way:

> Students entering Oakland Community College spend three hours taking a battery of tests. Some tests measure subtle abstractions, some measure visual and manual coordination, some index response of senses, and some indicate personal characteristics. The scores achieved on these tests and on demonstrable performances, along with supportive data from personal interviews, are translated into elements of the student's cognitive map—a picture of the ways he or she derives meaning from their environment and experiences.[3]

2. Ibid., p. 75.
3. Joseph Hill and Derik N. Nunney, "Career Mobility Through Personalized Occupational Education," *American Vocational Journal* 17, no. 3 (October 1971): 77.

Students' cognitive styles are determined by the way they take note of their total surroundings—how they seek meaning, how they become informed. Is the student a listener or a reader? Is he or she concerned only with his or her own viewpoint or is the student influenced in decision-making by family or associates? Does he or she reason in categories as a mathematician does or in relationships as social scientists do?

The students' cognitive maps help them and their counselors determine whether they would probably be better suited to learning chemistry in a classroom setting, by individual study with programmed materials, through informal conferences with other students, or by combining all these approaches in patterns that change from unit to unit during the course. The result is a "personalized educational prescription"—a suggested game plan intended to make the student's learning process as fruitful as possible.

An array of coordinated learning facilities helps broaden the student's options. Students whose cognitive style maps indicate they will progress fastest if they work at their own pace but with tutorial help might find the "individualized programmed learning laboratory" most useful. There they can use programmed texts, reading machines, films, and three-dimensional dynamic models. A faculty trained in individualized instruction methods is available to help with difficulties. A student who works best in an informal group may find the "carrel arcades" most conducive to learning. This approach offers audiovisual equipment which the student may use to view videotaped lectures and slides and to listen to instructional tapes. The program also offers talk sessions with other students, guided by a paraprofessional or a student tutor.

The student who comes alive in the dynamics of group interaction may participate in free-and-easy rap sessions with teachers and other students. The student who relates to teachers more easily on a one-to-one basis may work through conferences with the instructor. And students who work well with the help of more advanced students may be assigned to tutors. In practice, the cognitive style maps have produced up to nineteen ways of teaching the same course material, each one aimed at a particular kind of learning style.[4]

A cognitive style map, in addition to identifying the ways in which students can master an educational task most readily, gives them the self-knowledge essential to direct them to realistic career goals. Cognitive style is not immutable. It can be augmented. Missing strengths required for a specific occupation can be built onto a student's existing strengths.

COGNITIVE STYLES OF INNER-CITY CHILDREN

In everybody's style there are certain strengths. And everybody has an Achilles heel. In developing a significant change in learning one must control the Achilles heel and utilize the strengths. This is the central problem of the strategy of style, especially in its application to the inner-city pupils in our schools.

The following dimensions seem to characterize the cognitive style of many inner-city youngsters:

1. Strong development of nonaural senses such as the visual, tactile, and kinesthetic.
2. Well-developed nonverbal forms of communication such as gestures; less word-bound.
3. Greater expression in informal, unstructured, spontaneous situations.
4. Positive response to learning in cooperative settings such as children-teaching-children and youth-tutoring-youth designs.
5. Emphasis on learning from experience and action; a strong responsiveness to work-study programs, field-based learning, and action learning.[5]

Inner-city children have considerable facility with informal or public language, and this is expressed best in unstructured, spontaneous situations; they verbalize more freely around actions and things they can see; they understand more language than they speak; their nonverbal forms of expression are highly developed; and they often have imaginative and perceptive associations with words.

4. William Hampton, "Students Find Their Way to Learning with Cognitive Style Mapping," *College and University Business* 14, no. 1 (February 1972).

5. See Daniel R. Miller and Guy E. Swanson, *Inner Conflict and Defense* (New York: Henry Holt, 1960), p. 76.

Anyone who has worked with inner-city children knows that one of the surest ways to involve them in an activity is to make it into a game. For example, I know of teachers who have set up a mock court in the classroom to enable the class to discuss discipline, justice, and government in a meaningful way. Originally, the teachers had found it difficult to interest their children in these subjects, but the excitement of a make-believe court attracted considerable attention and provided a good beginning for discussion on a higher, more abstract level.

What is the source of the games orientation of inner-city children? Apparently, it is related to their down-to-earth, spontaneous approach to things. This extraverbal communication is usually called forth in games, most of which are not word-bound. Also, most games (not all, by any means) are person-centered and are generally concerned with direct action and visible results. Games are usually sharply defined and structured, with clear-cut goals. The rules are definite and can be readily absorbed. The inner-city child enjoys the challenge of the game and feels that he or she can do it.

But despite various types of latent creativity, inner-city children often fail to realize their potential because of lack of mastery of standard English. This is their Achilles heel.

The forms of communication characteristic of inner-city children raise important educational questions. The acquisition of knowledge obviously requires some degree of facility with formal language. As we have seen, inner-city children are capable of utilizing language in a rich and free fashion with well-developed nonverbal ways of communicating, but they lack skill in standard English. The problem for the educator is how to help them to attain this level of language so that their creative potential can be fully realized. It would be easy to say, as many people have, that we must give these children what most middle-class parents give their children—we must stimulate them in the use of language through reading, discussion, and the like. However, it is probable that this alone would not work, nor would it make the best use of inner-city children's particular mode of functioning. Their nonlinguistic skills should not be ignored or suppressed, but rather they should be brought out and integrated with verbal communication. The basic dimensions that characterize the cognitive style of inner-city youngsters should be built upon in the educational program. Inner-city children seem to learn best through games, role-playing, doing, seeing, talking, and learning in groups. These strengths can be captured and used to expand their reading and writing abilities without necessarily developing a reading or writing style.

Thus, it would seem essential that the method of teaching formal language to inner-city children take advantage of their communication style by employing teaching techniques that stress the visual, the physical, and the active as much as possible. We must be careful not to try to make these children over into replicas of middle-class children. The educational system should be pluralistic enough to find a place for a variety of learning styles.

6

Educational Programming: Strength vs. the Compensatory Approach

The basic compensatory approach that guided many of the large-scale educational efforts of the sixties carried with it an implicit message that almost guaranteed failure. The message said to the inner-city child: You are inadequate, you must shape up, I will give you the extra help to make you like me. The compensatory argument, in essence, leads from weakness and emphasizes deficiencies and deficits rather than strengths, positive attributes, and coping skills. The compensatory thesis expects less from the child and gets less. There have been numerous powerful criticisms of the whole compensatory programming with its emphasis on deficits, its attempts to make the child of the poor adapt to middle-class models, and so forth.[1]

Most of the compensatory programs of the sixties failed markedly, but currently there has developed what might be called an "intensive compensatory" model. In essence, in the new approach, the school zeroes in on a subject, say on reading, directing all its resources and personnel to improving the reading scores of inner-city children. But the approach still empha-

1. One of the best criticisms is to be found in Mario Fantini and Gerald Weinstein, *The Disadvantaged Child: Challenges to Education* (New York: Harper & Row, 1970).

88

sizes deficits and the children still hear the same message regarding their fundamental inadequacy. Because of their intensive and focused character, the current compensatory approaches may have slightly greater effectiveness than the more diffuse attacks of the sixties. I would argue, however, that their greatest potential lies in their becoming adjuncts of more positive approaches built on strengths.

If one analyzes the approaches that have been successful in improving the educational performance of inner-city children, one realizes that they are rooted in the strengths and the styles of the children rather than in a compensatory emphasis on deficiencies. In the context of building on strengths, reading deficits and the like can be overcome. While there are numerous approaches that either demonstrate or give promise of success, three overall designs stand out:

1. The use of various forms of what Fantini and Weinstein call *contact approaches.*[2]
2. The use of children teaching children (or youth tutoring youth), i.e., learning through teaching.
3. The use of educational assistants or paraprofessionals from the same background as the inner-city child.

Let us take a look at these in greater detail.

CONTACTING THE CHILD

There are two overall avenues for contacting the child—that is, connecting the child and the knowledge to be acquired. The first and most obvious is through the child's interests as they exist at the moment—the TV programs the child likes, the leaders he or she admires, such as Cesar Chavez or Muhammad Ali. As Fantini and Weinstein say, "the heart of teaching lies in reaching for the child's content, understanding its significance, and building upon it so that it becomes larger, and expands the child's frame of reference."[3] The second avenue is through the child's learning style, so that games, role playing, and trips are especially attractive to most inner-city children.

In the last two decades a great many programs have been

2. Ibid., p. 375.
3. Ibid., p. 376.

developed that incorporate the inner-city child's interests and styles; for example, the Urban League's Street Academy, Schools Without Walls, bilingual education, Jacksonville's Science-Fiction Film Reading Program, and many more. In addition, many techniques, approaches, and materials have been directed toward the same objective; for example, Sylvia Ashton Warner's "organics," action learning, much of the work of James Herndon, Herbert Kohl, and Jonathan Kozol, and so forth.

Fantini and Weinstein have also developed a number of specific approaches[4] toward contacting the inner-city child. Their book, *The Disadvantaged Child*, describes several of their programs, among them the following.

> One of the first assignments given to a group of urban teaching trainees was a "Pupils' Culture Survey." As part of this assignment, each trainee was to list some of his pupil's most often used slang expressions with illustrations of their usage. One trainee listed "bustin' suds," which, when translated, means "washing dishes." Such esoteric knowledge can often be utilized later, as illustrated by the following report from this trainee:
>
>> The sixth-grade class had just returned from lunch, and the teacher expended a considerable amount of energy in getting the pupils settled down. Then, one of her "troublemakers" walked in late. "Why are you late for class?" she asked. "I was bustin' suds," was the reply from the latecomer. The rest of the class became interested in the outcome of this exchange.
>>
>> "Well," the trainee said, "I'm sorry you had to wash the dishes but still that's no excuse for coming to class late. Now sit down and start your work." The boy's expression changed from amusement to surprise. "How did you know what bustin' suds meant?" "Oh, I get around," She replied smugly. "Now take your seat." He did and the class continued its work.
>
> Another teacher effectively utilized "Teach-Me" time. One period a week was set aside when the pupils were required to teach the teacher something they knew that he didn't. They would begin these periods by asking the teacher a series of Have-you-ever-heard-about. Whenever he pleaded ignorance, they would explain it to him. The topics ranged from the latest dance-step, to

4. Ibid. pp. 378–79.

a street game, to a pupil expression. This was not only an effective way for the teacher to learn his pupils' language and culture, but it also afforded him an opportunity to teach the pupils how to articulate more clearly their own experiences which they had taken for granted in more generalized form. Since the pupils tended to explain nonverbally, through facial expressions and gestures, the pupils were missing the value of explicit experiences. As the teacher gently and consistently prodded them to use words, they discovered that it was one thing to play stick-ball but quite another to tell someone how. Thus, both the teacher and his pupils learned from each other.

LEARNING THROUGH TEACHING

Let me turn now to another strength-based approach. There is mounting evidence that a very simple principle may provide a basic strategy for a leap in the learning of all children. That children learn from their peers is obvious, but a more significant observation is that children learn more from teaching other children. From this a major educational strategy follows—namely, that every child must be given the opportunity to play the teaching role, because it is through playing this role that he or she may really *learn how to learn*. In New York City a study found that over a five-month period in which older children tutored younger children with reading difficulties, those tutored gained 6.0 months while the tutors gained an extraordinary 3.4 years. A leap of this magnitude is the order of achievement that must be striven for in the schools of America.[5]

The key to learning is individualization, and the use of the student or pupil as a teacher is one way to increase this individualization. The concept of learning through teaching appears to be one of those basic ideas that do work, and it is finding a place in an enormous variety of settings, from the Youth Tutoring Youth programs of the National Commission on Resources for Youth and the cross-age learning experiments of the Lippitts to the Pocoima project in California, where the entire school is directed toward becoming a "tutorial community."

Children have been teaching other children throughout

5. See Alan Gartner, Mary Kohler, and Frank Riessman, *Children Teach Children* (New York: Harper & Row, 1971).

history, in manifold settings. The method occurred in one-room schoolhouses, it was central in the Lancaster system, and it is an important ingredient in the Montessori approach, in which the older, more advanced children are utilized to teach the younger, less advanced ones. In most of these programs, and in the early tutoring programs in the United States, the general emphasis has been on improving the learning of the recipient or tutee. The general finding has been that while the recipient may improve a small amount in his or her learning, there are no qualitative leaps, no breakthroughs or improvements of great magnitude on the cognitive indices utilized.

It was in the early sixties, however, that attention was focused on the potentially significant benefits that may accrue to the tutor. Working at Mobilization for Youth, I observed the rather extensive tutoring program that had been established, in which high school youngsters were trained to tutor disadvantaged elementary school youngsters who were doing poorly in school. It seemed from impressional observations that while the tutees enjoyed the tutoring sessions, there was no great improvement in their learning. What increasingly stood out, on the other hand, was that the tutors really appeared to be "turned on" by what they were doing. They not only were excited about it, and derived a new, heightened self-esteem from it, but they also seemed much more interested in the whole learning process.

The tutors seemed further to acquire a new attitude toward learning, and new skills, and perhaps even more important, new awareness of learning and studying. In a sense they were beginning to learn how to learn and to manage their own learning. They were acquiring new learning "sets," and there were indications that these new sets or skills and new attitudes were beginning to be transferred to the many different learning experiences in which the students were involved. Thus, a tutor who was teaching arithmetic to an elementary school youngster appeared to show improvement in mathematics and in many subjects other than mathematics as well. More than that, in many cases the tutors seemed to acquire a new, self-conscious, analytic orientation in dealing with all kinds of problems, not just academic work.

These observations led Mobilization for Youth's research

staff, in particular Robert Cloward and his associates, to develop carefully controlled studies to assess what was occurring. They found striking gains in the achievement scores of the tutors, gains that far exceeded those of the tutees. Unfortunately, most of the cognitive measures that were employed, not only at MFY but elsewhere, have thus far been largely restricted to achievement tests. There is a great need to develop new, expanded indices related to learning sets, creativity, learning how to learn, analytic thinking, curiosity, and the like.[6]

There is increasing recognition today that learning need not be a win/lose game in which some pupils presumably learn a good deal in a competitive grading system and others do not. There is a need for what William Glasser calls Schools Without Failure. In the learning through teaching (LTT) design it is possible for all children to learn effectively through the process of teaching other children, and learning can therefore become a much more worthwhile game. It may be possible, then, to move from the present nonindividualized and competitive system to an individualized and cooperative one.

It is rare for older youngsters to have the opportunity to play a constructive, socializing, positive role with younger children, but the cross-age model allows for and greatly encourages this. LTT may play an important role in combating prejudice. It is especially intriguing to think of the possibilities of Blacks helping whites, of younger children helping older ones, of ethnic minority members helping the majority.

Some of the same principles that are operative in LTT may function in a wide variety of other settings, especially in the rapidly expanding self-help movement. I noted in formulating the "helper therapy principle" that:

> People with a problem helping other people who have the same problem in more severe form (e.g., Alcoholics Anonymous), is a simple age-old approach, well-known to all group therapists. But in using this approach—and there is a marked current increase in its use—we may be placing the emphasis on the wrong person in centering attention on the individual receiving the help. More

6. See Gartner, Kohler, and Riessman, *Children Teach Children*, for more evaluation studies of the learning-through-teaching principle, especially Appendix 3, pp. 151 and 153.

attention might well be given . . . to the person who is providing the assistance—the helper—because it is he who really improves!

While it may be uncertain that people receiving help are always benefited, it seems much clearer that the people giving the help are profiting from their role. This appears to be the case in a wide variety of group "therapies," including Synanon (for drug addicts), Recovery Incorporated (for psychologically disturbed people), Alcoholics Anonymous (for alcoholics). Perhaps, then, our strategy ought to be to devise ways of creating more helpers. Or to be more exact, how to transform receivers of help into dispensers of help; how to reverse their roles, how to structure the situation so that receivers of help will be placed in roles requiring the giving of assistance.[7]

Of course, the "helper therapy principle" has been formulated in contexts where the helper is in some way deficient and gains from the helping. This is not necessarily the case in learning through teaching, which can benefit all children, deficient or not. The common bond uniting these two programs is the power of the helping mechanism in its effect upon the person playing the helper role.

There are a great many different reasons at both the emotional and the cognitive levels why learning through teaching is effective. It is because it is effective at so many different levels and through so many different mechanisms that the principle acquires its enormous power and potential.

Because helping other children to learn and playing the helper role are exciting and novel, they may provide an excellent contact to learning. But perhaps even more important, the principle may assist the child tutor to learn how to learn, which is a much deeper dimension of the learning process and one that may carry multiplying effects. If one learns how to learn, one can be a learner in a great number of areas. In order to teach another child material, a child needs to learn the material better in the first place; he or she needs to organize it, needs to observe another learner and make contact with that learner. In essence, he or she must become a manager of learning and

7. Frank Riessman, "The Helper Therapy Principle," *Social Work* 12, no. 3 (April 1965): 17–24.

become more aware of learning; all this contributes to learning how to learn.

In a sense, learning through teaching is an illustration of role theory; an individual playing a new role, whether it be the teacher role or the helper role in a therapeutic context, develops new behavior patterns related to that role, acquires new experiences, new feelings, new consciousness. The role playing may unleash new energies in the child and build his or her self-concept—"I must be fairly good if I can help somebody else"—and the competence acquired from giving this help furthers the development and self-confidence.

The evidence indicates that learning through teaching or children teaching children is a highly effective method of improving the learning of the tutor, again as measured by a variety of indicators in both the cognitive and effective areas. For this program to become fully effective it needs to be more highly institutionalized and the logistics of the program need to be carefully planned with full involvement of teacher, parents, children, administrators, and other school personnel. Moreover, there is no reason why the tutee in the learning through teaching model could not learn more effectively (the evidence thus far indicates that the tutee progresses enormously). Apart from the general suggestion that all children in school should have the opportunity to play the teacher or tutor role, we can recommend that schools utilize material that promises greater success for the tutee's learning. Such a program is now being developed by New Dimensions in Education by using their Alpha series, which has been highly successful in the teaching of reading. By adapting this technique so that tutors can use it in the teaching of reading to younger children, we may make it possible for both the tutor and the tutee to achieve a leap in learning.

THE ROLE OF PARAPROFESSIONALS

Two well-designed studies present important data on the work and effects of paraprofessionals in schools. The first study —conducted by Eaton Conant of the University of Oregon, under a grant from the U.S. Office of Education—found that the use of aides in the first through fourth grades of the Portland,

Oregon schools brought increased instructional time to the children—from both the aide and the teacher. The study also found that teacher/aide teams delivered instruction at a lower per-hour cost than teachers alone, and the use of paraprofessionals had a favorable effect upon pupil learning.[8] Findings of the Oregon study are summarized below.

During a five-hour day, teachers alone in classrooms spent 92 minutes on instructional activities. With the introduction of an aide, teachers' time in instruction rose to 109 minutes, with the aide providing an additional 129 minutes of instructional activity.

Average total costs for an hour of instruction by a teacher/aide team were $8.80, compared with over $16 for a teacher alone. These differences were largely attributable to the additional instruction provided by both teacher and aide and the lower costs of paraprofessionals.

The program had its greatest effect in raising the achievement levels of Black children.

In the second survey, over 3,500 paraprofessionals in New York City were studied by the Institute for Educational Development. The key findings related to the substantive instructional work done by the paraprofessionals and the strong positive evaluation given to their work by teachers, principals, and students alike.

The most common paraprofessional work activities were talking quietly with a child who was upset or disturbing the class, stopping arguments or fights among students, assisting with learning drills in reading or mathematics, going over a paper with children, and listening to children tell stories.

More than 90 percent of the pupils interviewed said that they enjoyed coming to school more since the paraprofessionals were working in the school; principals and teachers said that pupil attitudes had improved and attendance had increased; and parents reported that their children were more interested in schoolwork.

Teachers described the major effect of paraprofessionals as

8. See *New Human Services Newsletter* 1, no. 4 (1972). For a full discussion see Alan Gartner, *Paraprofessionals and Their Performance* (New York: Praeger, 1971).

an increase in pupils' academic achievement. In noting the broad range of persons who successfully held the paraprofessional positions, the study stated that "there are few limits on the kinds of people who can perform satisfactorily as paraprofessionals."[9]

Studies in Indiana, Minnesota, Colorado, and New York indicate more specifically the effect of paraprofessionals on pupil learning. In Minneapolis, pupil learning—as measured by pretest pairs using the Metropolitan Reading Readiness Test given at five-month intervals to 234 children—was 50 percent greater in kindergarten classes with a paraprofessional than in classes without an aide.[10] Similar gains were shown in number readiness.

In Greenburgh, New York, performances of second-grade classes with an aide were compared with similar classes the previous school year that had no paraprofessionals. The measuring instrument was the Metropolitan Achievement Test. The number of classes scoring above grade level increased from two to five and those scoring below grade level decreased from five to four. The project's director states that the introduction of the teacher's aide was responsible for this achievement test outcome.[11] And in Greeley, Colorado, in a Title III ESEA (Elementary and Secondary Education Act) program, where demonstrable pupil performance gains were achieved, the teachers attribute these gains primarily to the introduction of paraprofessionals.[12]

A study conducted by Greenleigh Associates for OEO (Office of Economic Opportunity) to ascertain the most effective remedial reading program found that in each of the systems tested the most effective teacher was a paraprofessional rather than a regular teacher or a certified remedial reading teacher. Another study, this one conducted by the psychology department of Indiana University, examined a tutoring pro-

9. *New Human Services Newsletter* 1, no. 4 (1972).

10. Minneapolis Public Schools, "Teacher Aide Project," Minneapolis, Minn., 1968, p. 17.

11. Project description, National Conference on Paraprofessionals, Career Advancement, and Pupil Learning, January 9, 1969, p. 3.

12. PACE, "Exemplary Education for Early Childhood," Weld County School District, Greeley, Col., July 1968, p. 23.

gram where paraprofessionals who were trained for a total of twenty-one hours are successfully tutoring first-grade children for fifteen minutes a day, five days a week, in some fifty projects in twelve states. The study has shown decisive improvement in the reading performance on the part of the children.[13]

Finally, a Florida program that trained fifteen women to work with preschool children has produced a marked effect upon the children's development of a variety of skills. The project, Early Child Stimulation Through Parent Education, conducted at the College of Education of the University of Florida under a HEW (Department of Health, Education, and Welfare) Children's Bureau research grant, found that this type of program does have a clear payoff in enhanced development of the infants whose mothers are reached in their homes.[14] The parent educators, themselves "disadvantaged," worked with nearly three hundred mothers and their children. The major work of the parent educators was instructing the mothers in a series of stimulation exercises designed to provide physical, intellectual, and social stimulation for the children, whose ages ranged from three months to two years. On a standard measure of assessment (the Griffiths Mental Development Scale), the children whose mothers were so trained performed better on all scales—locomotor, personal-social, hearing and speech, eye and hand, and general performance—than did those in a matched control group whose parents did not receive this training.

The overall evidence indicates that the use of paraprofessionals leads to a definite improvement in the learning of children. This effect can be greatly enhanced by emphasizing the educational function of the paraprofessional, increasing paraprofessional training, and restructuring the roles of the teacher and the educational assistant. The paraprofessional program, which is career oriented and allows the teacher's aide to move through such various stages as teacher assistant, teacher associate, and teacher while working full-time, is particularly effective.

13. Project description, National Conference on Paraprofessionals, p. 7.
14. Alan Gartner, *Do Paraprofessionals Improve Human Services?* (New York: New Careers Development Center, 1969), p. 18.

In the national Career Opportunities Program (COP) this effectiveness has been demonstrated. According to almost every indicator employed, the COP paraprofessionals become excellent teachers, learning on the job and acquiring education in released time.[15]

There are probably a number of mechanisms whereby the paraprofessional improves the educational achievement of children:

1. The teacher is freed to spend more time teaching.
2. There is more individualized teaching and learning, and a decentralizing of the classroom.
3. A second adult gives the child an alternate person to relate to, to work with, and to use as a model.

There is a growing body of data which indicates that paraprofessionals allow teachers time to give more individualized attention to children and to prepare better both in school and at home. The fact that the teacher's audience now includes another adult appears to encourage greater preparatory efforts on the teacher's part.[16]

The involvement of paraprofessionals, apart from their direct impact on the learning of their pupils, has other indirect potential effects. These adults now provide very different models for their own children, who may have been experiencing difficulty in school. Various studies of paraprofessional programs indicate that the paraprofessionals' school know-how increases and, thus, they are better able to help their children make their way through the system. Also, the aspirations of other community members are raised as they see their neighbors doing varied work, and attending college. And the aspirations of the paraprofessionals themselves are increased. In a sense, they become more like the traditional parent who has "made it" and values education.

In addition to the paraprofessionals, of course, there are increasing numbers of people in the inner city who are acquir-

15. See William Smith, "Career Opportunities Program," COP Bulletin no. 3, New Careers Training Laboratory, 1973, p. 5.

16. "Teacher Aides: Handbook for Instructors and Administrators," University Extension, University of Wisconsin, Madison, 1968.

ing higher education via continuing education programs, external degrees, open enrollment, and so on. Apart from the potential value to the individuals themselves, these activities offer the
possibility that the parents may become a new kind of model
for their children and thereby positively affect the children's
learning.

There is another pathway for inner-city parents to affect
their children's school performance, at least indirectly. This is
through participatory community involvement in the schools,
for example, on school boards. Community involvement is directed at transforming the schools and making them more educationally appropriate for the youngsters by changing the curriculum, the personnel, and the procedures. This is the direct
and manifest intention of community involvement, but it has
another, indirect effect which should be noted in connection
with the strategy I am outlining. Parents who are involved in
their schools provide a new parental model, a model that says
to the child that school and learning are important, that we, the
parents, are tremendously involved in it, and that you are very
capable of learning. The parents, then, become counterparts of
the middle-class parents in other communities who are constantly concerned with school matters.

BEYOND THE CONTACT CURRICULUM: STAGES IN THE LEARNING PROCESS

While the evidence for the effectiveness of paraprofessionals and children teaching children is compelling, the reports on
various contact approaches is more impressional and anecdotal,
and depends more on affective than on cognitive indicators.
Thus the reported responses to the use of films, role-playing
games, and the like, typically note that "discipline" problems
decline, the children are awakened, focused, and interested,
they like the class, and so forth. These reports do not usually
indicate any significant reading achievement gains, and this is
understandable because the purpose of the contact approach is
to connect the body of knowledge that is to be taught with the
child's interests and/or style. The purpose is not to impart much
knowledge nor to develop skills. Thus the use of the contact
approach is an extremely important *first step* in learning—a

step which is often missed or quickly disposed of in the learning process. The connection of the curriculum and the child's interests is actually a slow process that in no way develops systematic learning. In the last decade a great many contact approaches have been developed and a good percentage of teachers probably are aware of many of them and do succeed in varying degrees in contacting the child. Unfortunately, many teachers do not go beyond this contact stage and so they wind up essentially entertaining the children, holding their interest but not developing their learning power.

Ultimately the children must progress through a number of stages if they are to become really educated. Children must learn how to learn, and become self-conscious about the learning process, acquire skills and knowledge and learn in some depth the structure of a field or subject. This last requires not only learning skill and knowledge, but some ability to learn what is not immediately relevant or interesting, to suspend relevance, so to speak, in order to learn the basic subject matter in a systematic, disciplined fashion. In essence, this type of learning, which is much more like traditional education, more cognitive and less affective, is the antithesis of contact learning, which is more progressive, affective, open-ended, unorganized. The fully educated child must profit from the benefits of both progressive and traditional education, integrated in a new amalgam.

In order to achieve this integration, it may be useful to develop a phased strategy which perhaps moves from contact to learning how to learn in a second stage, to the acquisition of basic skills in a third stage, and eventuating at the fourth stage in understanding of the basic structure of a subject in a systematic manner. Obviously the stages overlap and approaches and techniques can be used differently, depending upon which stage is being accented. Thus the cognitive style can be applied as part of the contact curriculum, but it also can be used to help the child learn how to learn. The discovery method can be used as an aid in developing learning and as a contacter. Computer-assisted programmed instruction can be used once a child has been contacted in order to develop basic skills and knowledge, but also as a kind of gimmick in developing contact as well as a more fully structured understanding of a field. Learning through teaching or children teaching children may be used as a method for learning how to learn, and as a contact device for "turning on" the child. Action learning can be used as a contact method but may also be useful in learning how to learn. Strength-based approaches are probably particularly useful in the contact stage and in learning how to learn, but ultimately, of course, weaknesses have to be recognized, diagnosed, and overcome or limited in order to move on to a higher stage of learning.

Naturally, it is not necessary to accept the sequencing of the learning process that I have outlined, but unless some phasing strategy is consciously employed, large numbers of children, particularly inner-city children, are likely to remain at the contact stage at best, and advanced learning will remain accidental and chaotic. One of the major errors of the modern school system is its attempt to move too quickly to the advanced stage of traditional learning, its demand that the youngsters acquire skills and systematic knowledge without ever having been contacted. The result for the inner-city child is generally a total dislike for school, while for the middle-class child this leads to the learning of subjects in a rote fashion.

While the use of paraprofessionals, children teaching children, and other innovative techniques has important benefits for the learning of children, each in its own right, perhaps the key to a major leap in learning technology would be the integration of these strength-based approaches into an overall educational design in which each approach is used self-consciously to its fullest extent. The California Early Childhood Program represents one attempt at such an integration. Below is an evaluation of the program's use of paraprofessionals and children teaching children (here referred to as "cross-age tutors"):

1. There was a significant decrease in the adult-to-pupil ratio as a result of the utilization of paid aides, volunteer aides, and cross-age tutors. The ratio dropped from 1 to 6.54 in 1972–73 to 1 to 2.90 in 1973–74.
2. More than 85 percent of the respondents reported a significant positive change in student attitude as a result of the use of aides and cross-age tutors. Less than 1 percent reported any negative change in attitude.

3. More than one-half of the respondents reported a decrease in the number of referrals for disciplinary reasons, which they attributed to the use of aides.
4. In the opinion of the respondents, nearly 100 percent of the teachers in schools in which they served as principals somewhat favored or strongly favored the use of aides.
5. Nearly 93 percent of the respondents indicated that district-wide teacher organizations somewhat favored or strongly favored the use of differentiated staffing as implemented in ECE schools.
6. In response to community surveys, respondents reported that 89 percent of the parents and members of the school community strongly favored the use of paid aides in ECE classrooms.[17]

These approaches are not only educationally beneficial, they are also economical. Without expanding the school budget, it may be possible to achieve a far better ratio of adults to children in the classroom and thus increase the possibility of more individualized instruction.

17. Norman Guith, "A Doctoral Study of Differential Staffing in California's ECE Schools," *Phi Delta Kappan,* September 1975, p. 7.

7

Strategies for Accountability

Currently, and for the last five years for that matter, a major strategy for achieving accountability in education has been the development of CBTE (Competency-Based Teacher Education and Competency-Based Teacher Evaluation). While accepting the fact that CBTE has drawn our attention to actual teachers' competencies in the classroom rather than to abstract credentials, I propose that we look to learning approaches that give promise of definitive improvement in children's learning as measured by a wide variety of criteria, both cognitive and affective, and that we then attempt to integrate these approaches and institute them in our educational programming. (An approach to the institutionalization of good practice is proposed in Chapter 8.)

Educators who are zealous advocates of competency-based teacher education as the one and only educational strategy for the future have begun to lose sight of the fact that the value of CBTE, like that of any other educational program, must be measured in terms of its effects on children's learning. While the strength of the CBTE movement lies in its call for accountability, it has had the effect of focusing all eyes on teacher performance rather than on student progress. Because of this, CBTE has enormous possibilities as a diversion. The vast proliferation of performance criteria has already begun to obfuscate our primary goal: the reorganization of the teaching/learning experience so that children learn.

While many CBTE proponents have accepted as a given

that teacher training and teacher behavior are critical for the learning of children, there is surprisingly little empirical evidence to support this assertion. It may well be that school administrators are the key agents of change and utilizing paraprofessionals may be a more important factor in improving children's learning. Although most of the data seems to be impressional, there is increasing evidence that the principal of the school, rather than the teacher, may be the strategic agent in the improvement of learning.[1] Much more attention needs to be given to the training and retraining of principals, as well as superintendents and administrators, instead of our preoccupation with the training (and scapegoating) of teachers.

The principal's role as a change agent has two dimensions: first, as the implementer of change that has been specified by the school system, and second, as the innovator of change within his or her school. I have seen a number of schools where the change of a principal—unaccompanied by any other change—has led to a remarkable modification in teacher practice, children's learning, attendance, morale, parent involvement, and so on, all from teachers, students, and parents who were performing much more inadequately prior to the introduction of the new principal. In the context of this new role for the principal, the training of teachers can take place in a new setting. The teacher of tomorrow should be much more of a "little principal"—an orchestrator or manager utilizing other personnel including paraprofessionals and specialists, managing small groups, organizing learning-through-teaching programs, and so forth.

Teachers should also have the alternative of moving up to become "master teachers" rather than having to move over to an administrative line as the only form of advancement. Teachers need to be recruited in different fashions, perhaps by first becoming paraprofessionals as in the Career Opportunities Program of the U.S. Office of Education (COP), rather than going the traditional route of education first and experience later.

We must recognize too that teachers have vastly different

1. See Seymour B. Sarason, *The Culture of the School and the Problem of Change* (Boston: Allyn and Bacon, 1971), and William W. Wayson, "A New Kind of Principal," in *The National Elementary Principal* 6, no. 4 (February 1971).

styles and we should capitalize upon these rather than reduce teaching behavior to a series of competencies. We need to look more at which teachers are successful in improving the learning of children (measured in a variety of ways), rather than merely look at their abstract competencies, which may not affect children's learning. Although a cliché, it is a well-known observation that there are certain teachers in every school who do remarkably well in affecting the learning of their pupils; perhaps their methodology and style should be studied and fully utilized.

Teachers must also learn to control their "teacher's reflex," which functions to reward and reinforce children in the teacher's own image, and they need to emphasize new learning in children rather than the reinforcement of what the child already knows. (It is my impression that considerable "teaching" is in the latter category.) Finally, we need a new approach to the development and evaluation of productivity in the school. The remainder of this chapter is devoted to this issue.

PRODUCTIVITY AND EVALUATION ISSUES

Education is faced with the interrelated challenge of cost and productivity. Generally, the cost issue has come to the fore as concerns about the lack of productivity have mounted. It would seem likely that were productivity increased—were children learning more—then the taxpayers would be more willing to carry the costs of education.

Children are commonly seen as the ultimate beneficiaries of educational programs. Here I want to suggest that they are the key to productivity increases as well, and, this being the case, that the management of educational programs must be built upon recognition of the child as a producer of his or her own learning. Traditionally we think of productivity as a function of technology—the more machinery, the more efficient production will be. This has certainly been characteristic of the manufacturing of goods. On the other hand, education is labor-intensive; that is, it uses a high proportion of labor or human power in contrast to machinery or capital in order to produce the service or product. To make education more efficient, it has seemed natural to try to mechanize it more; that is, to apply

machinery so that it will perhaps become more like manufacturing.

Traditional notions argue that productivity in education
cannot be increased sharply because it is not amenable to capi-
tal-intensive inputs; moreover, as it is labor-intensive, the work
inputs are costly and potentially inflationary. My point, however, is that education and all human service work is *consumer-
intensive* and the key to increasing productivity in this sector
lies in effectively engaging and mobilizing the consumer—the
child.

The fact is that there are very few examples of marked
advances in output in the service spheres, but fortunately there
are a few, and perhaps something can be learned from a look
at them. Of course, there is the problem of definition. What,
after all, is a marked improvement in service delivery, and how
is it to be assessed? As a working model, I would suggest the
following indices:

1. An advance in output of a magnitude that is significant and
   enduring; e.g., children's reading scores improving 30 percent
   or more, and remaining at the new level.
2. The rapid spread in the utilization of a service of "obvious"
   value; e.g., use of students as teachers and tutors.
3. A strong positive subjective report by users of a service where
   the subjective element may be said to be the decisive variable;
   e.g., students reporting positive change in their attitude toward
   school.
4. Changes in behavior at multiple levels; in education, for example, changes in both the cognitive and affective dimensions.
      Thus, if in the process of learning to read a child acquires
   a more cooperative attitude and a feeling of greater power,
   these added outputs (frequently emanating from the context of
   the service) can be seen as important reflections of the value of
   the educational service.

With these criteria in mind, some actual illustrations can be
cited. The discussion in Chapter 6 illustrates a marked change
in output where children are utilized to teach other children.
Here the older children who do the tutoring have been observed to achieve a dramatic advance in their own learning—
as much as three years in reading improvement in six months'
time. These changes have been lasting and are typically accom-

panied by changes in attitude toward learning, increased self-confidence, and the like.

A second illustration can be found in various applications of the self-help movement. For example, it has been reported that the most effective approaches to weight control are the various weight watchers groups—and to a lesser extent this seems to be true for smokers, alcoholics, and drug addicts, although the data are more ambiguous than in weight reduction. Of added importance is the fact that these behaviors have been very resistant to change by all other methods.

CONSUMER-INTENSIVE SERVICES

What these examples seem to have in common, in addition to the fact that they are inexpensive, is a special involvement of "consumers," so that they become a force in the increase of the productivity of the service. The consumers are performing specific functions in the delivery of the service, not some general form of participation. And there is a definite increase in the output: learning and/or an extension of the service.

Here, then, is a decisive factor which can affect education. If we see students, for example, not as the passive recipients of teaching but as *workers in the production of their own learning,* then the organization of those learning activities takes on a quite different focus. What is essential in efforts to increase children's learning, then, is adoption of those activities that can enlist the student as a more active and effective learner/worker. Helping students to learn will make them more effective and efficient learners in the future. Engaging students in a program where they learn through teaching other students makes most efficient use of the student/worker. If students are a key factor in the production of their own learning, then the other forces of production, such as teachers and equipment, must be directed toward maximizing the efficiency of the student. One of the ways to do this is to give students a say in what is to be learned and how the learning is to be organized. If this is done, then the students are more likely to be motivated to work hard—that is, to be effective producers of their own learning.

Some of the steps that may be taken in education can be seen by looking at designs developed for the improvement of the productivity of other types of workers. Much attention has been given in recent years to improving the productivity and satisfaction of factory workers by developing teams to reduce worker isolation, rotating assembly-line workers so as to give a sense of wholeness to their efforts, and giving workers control of some or all of the manufacturing operations to produce a feeling of autonomy and involvement. These same principles apply to efforts to improve the quality of work performed by students as a factor in producing their own learning. For example, the work (learning) must be interesting; it should be carried on so that the worker (student) can have positive relationships with co-workers (other students and teachers); there should be an apparent connection between the various parts of the work; the relationship of the particular job (the item being studied) to the larger enterprise (the student's entire learning) should be real and clear; and the worker (student) should have some discretion and control over what he or she does—the order, pace, and content of the work.

I am not suggesting the removal of the teacher or other professional. Rather I would propose new roles in which the teacher may be the catalyst, manager, and supervisor who directs skills and know-how toward the maximum involvement of the student, not merely for the sake of student participation and all that may mean in emotional terms, but also to improve the quality of the learning. The training and managerial skills of the teacher will have to be quite different from what they are today, and will have to be focused outward upon the students. The teacher will have to be directed toward involving students and organizing the system so that it will encourage better student input. Thus, in a school that plans to have all the children teach other children, there are special problems of logistics as well as issues related to preparing the children, parents, and others for this new program. The actual process of children teaching children is not complicated, but the organization of it for maximal efficiency is quite another matter.

PARTICIPATION IS NOT ENOUGH

It is important to understand the role of the community in providing the context for improved learning. If the community has a say in what is to be learned, who is to be employed, and how the learning is to be organized, then it is likely that the students will be much more involved in the school and motivated to work hard—that is, to be effective producers in their own learning. However, while community participation is an antecedent to the kind of consumer input I have been describing, it is not sufficient in and of itself. People may participate without any improvement in their learning; they may not become engaged in teaching themselves, learning how to learn, listening more carefully, or any of the cognitive mechanisms related to a jump in performance. In many cases, the participation may be a detour; although it may be valuable on its own terms, it may fail to lead to increased learning. Hence it is important that we give careful attention to the mechanisms of connecting participation or any other approach to expanded consumer involvement in the actual performance of the function.

Most of what I am suggesting is not new, of course. Making learning self-directing, giving the students and their community a role in the school, increasing the students' motivation, are all well-known ideas. What I am suggesting is that these and similar efforts need to be recast in the context of seeing students as the key factors in their own learning. By enlisting the student as a force in the production of learning and by focusing other inputs so as to facilitate this role, the product of the work—the student's learning—will be maximized.

This approach is potentially highly economical in that it vastly expands the service resources of the system and thereby increases the productivity of the producer—that is, the teacher. This is quite a different model, however, from the current approach to increasing productivity of teachers—for example, by having them teach more students. The danger in the latter practice is that the teaching may become less effective; the teacher may be teaching more but not teaching better.

THE PROBLEM OF EVALUATION

Central to both the approach discussed above and the larger-scale efforts to reshape education is the issue of evaluation.

The problem of evaluation of education is enormous.[2] Let us look at a few examples. If we use achievement or reading test scores to assess the effectiveness of teachers, we are faced with the problem that the teachers may then "teach to the test."[3] And in extreme cases they may actually provide the tests in advance. If we utilize a measure of the student's self-concept as a way of evaluating some educational intervention, the question arises, has his or her self-concept improved while cognitive performance remained the same? If we use the teacher's judgment of what has been happening to the work of the pupils, there is an obvious potential for bias, as the teacher may want to indicate that he or she is doing a good job. An outside independent judge may be less capable of assessing what is going on every day or may obtain a restricted performance on the day of evaluation. On and on go the limitations.

In many cases, faced with the problems of evaluation those who are supposed to do the evaluating simply decide not to do it, pleading how hard it is. Or the evaluators develop such superfine instruments that they find that little has, in fact, occurred (or, more precisely, little that their instruments can measure). Another alternative is that recognizing this last problem, evaluators seek out only gross and impressional results. None of these alternatives is acceptable.

Rather we need an evaluation model that employs multiple indices, each different from the other, each having different weaknesses and strengths that may countervail each other, but converging toward a similar result or assessment. In the psychological literature, this is termed *convergent* or *discriminant validity*. Thus, in the case of a psychotherapeutic intervention, if the patient, his or her friends, relatives, fellow employees,

2. For a superb discussion of evaluation and a powerful critique of standardized testing see *Principal* 54, no. 6 (July–August 1975).

3. A basic problem of all standardized reading tests is that the student is rated comparatively in terms of national norms rather than according to whether he or she can actually read effectively. An approach that gives promise, although relatively untested thus far, is called "criterion reference tests of reading skills." Criterion reference tests are used to assess student achievement in terms of a criterion standard. These tests furnish information about the degree of competence reached by the individual learner and are independent of reference to the performance of other learners or national norms.

supervisors, psychiatrists, and perhaps an independent judge agree that he or she has progressed markedly, we may be more persuaded than if any one of them alone so indicated. If, further, there is some measure such as a projective test that also indicates progress, we are further reassured. If, in addition, there are some major behavioral changes in the patient's life, such as being able to graduate from college after failing previously, this may be further evidence that the intervention is meaningful. To repeat, no one of these indices alone would be sufficient, and of course we can't always have all the indicators working uniformly in the same direction, so we would need to develop some fairly acceptable pattern of indices.

There are a number of other factors that we might want to consider in our evaluation schema. First, we will want changes to be relatively enduring and not due to any such effect as the Hawthorne. Then, we might be particularly concerned that the changes be of a large qualitative type; for example, children progressing three years in their reading scores in six months, as has occurred in some youth-tutoring-youth programs.

In the evaluation of education or any human service technique, it is important to distinguish the direct effect from the more indirect consequences of the technique. For example, one must distinguish between the improvement in learning and the way it is presented or whether it is cooperative or collegial or independent, or whatever. By confusing these dimensions, we not only fail to measure the more indirect dimension, which may have more far-reaching, long-range effects, but we often automatically assume that the two dimensions are working in the same direction. This, of course, may be true, but it requires more direct evaluation procedures, utilizing multiple indices, for us to be sure.

Finally, there are special evaluation questions related to the fact that some approaches are good for some people and some groups, and not for others: individual differences, style differences, and subgroup differences are extremely important. The open classroom may work very well for some kinds of youngsters, particularly those who have already developed an interest in learning, and yet be very inappropriate for other groups. Similarly, the contact curriculum may be a complete waste of time for youngsters who are already deeply involved in learning. Role playing may be a useful approach with some children and be counterindicated with others. Some teachers may use games very effectively, while others function better with a more structured lesson. This is not to say that everything eventually works, but rather that there are many paths to learning, many different approaches and styles that may be effective, and this adds further to the evaluation problem.

8

Instituting Large-Scale
Educational Reform

The charge is being made on many sides that schools are irrelevant—that the amount of money spent, the educational practice utilized, the segregation or desegregation of the school, and so forth, have no effect on the learning of children. The argument has had great impact in recent years, spearheaded by the ideological criticism of Ivan Illich and buttressed by the large-scale national studies of James Coleman and Christopher Jencks.[1]

Yet despite these data, as I have indicated throughout this book, there are numerous studies, experiments, and demonstrations which clearly indicate that a particular teaching practice, or the use of new personnel such as paraprofessionals, or a new curriculum can have a decisive and measurable effect on children's learning. But these experiments have not been carried over into the educational system on a large scale. For example, Martin Deutsch has successfully demonstrated that stimulus enrichment for inner-city children in the early years has a striking effect on their cognitive development, later learning, and IQ even when they return to the standard school setting.[2] But

1. See also an unpublished report by the Organization for Economic Cooperative Development, 1969, which summarizes the European experience and research indicating that expended funds and changed class ratio and educational policy do not affect educational outcomes.
2. Marshall A. Smith and Joan S. Bissell, "Report Analysis: The Impact of Head Start," *Harvard Educational Review* 40, no. 1 (February 1970): 51–104.

in the nationwide Head Start program no such results were found.[3] Alan Gartner has cited a good number of studies where the utilization of paraprofessionals in schools has led to definite improvements in learning, reading scores, and so forth, on the part of children.[4] But there is no evidence that the large-scale use of paraprofessionals in the United States has had a major effect on the learning of children. And there are countless experiments showing that the IQ can be dramatically improved in a very short period of time, in some cases in as little as three to five days, while again there is no evidence that any large-scale program has had similar effects.[5] The Urban League's street academy approach has been highly effective with disadvantaged youngsters. But again, this program has not been developed on a national scale. Thus the results of these innovative programs are left isolated and do not show up in the findings reported by Jencks, Coleman, and others.

THE ROLE OF DEMONSTRATION EXPERIMENTS

The issue, of course, is how these two sets of apparently contradictory data can both be true. How can it be correct, as Coleman, Jencks, and others argue, that school factors, collectively and individually, have little effect upon children, while studies such as those cited above show marked and significant results? The big factor, of course, relates to the very character of the two assessments; namely, that the Coleman, Jencks, and similar studies are surveys of large universes, using gross measures, able to detect only broad effects across a wide spectrum of subjects. On the other hand, the studies that have shown positive results look at specific projects, often limited in time, always circumscribed in a target population; in short, they are experiments or demonstrations of small order that typically have not been institutionalized. The need then is to analyze some of the reasons why the experimental and demonstration results have not been carried over into institutional change.

3. Ibid.

4. Alan Gartner, *Paraprofessionals and Their Performance: A Survey of Education, Health and Social Service Programs* (New York: Praeger, 1971).

5. Ernest A. Haggard, "Social Status and Intelligence," *Genetic Psychology Monographs* 49, no. 4 (1954): 141–86; also personal communication from Dr. Haggard.

In some cases the results that are produced in a demonstration may be unique and not easily translatable to a national scale. The reasons for this may be that there was powerful, charismatic leadership in the demonstration program; that utilizing such a tremendous overload of personnel and other resources was so expensive that it would not be economical on a large scale; or that some special conditions, such as the selection of "creamed" populations or exceptionally trained and dedicated personnel, were involved.

There are, however, features of the demonstration that may have some interesting applicability at the large-scale level. For example, typically in a demonstration traditional rules are modified or suspended, commitment to the project is considerable, concentration on a particular result is evident, and funding is sufficient. Lest one believe, however, that there are only favorable aspects about new programs and demonstrations, it should be pointed out that many demonstrations fail, and there are many factors working against success in any new venture. A new program charting unknown, unfamiliar paths evokes a natural resistance, since it is upsetting the tradition, the equilibrium, and the stability of established ways. Because the demonstration or experiment is new, there are also likely to be a considerable number of unanticipated negative consequences which, unless they are overcome, will lead to the failure of the demonstration.

The point is that in the institutionalization of an idea that has been demonstrated there are often advantages which the demonstration itself did not have. The demonstration, if successful, has presumably overcome some of the difficulties; the territory is no longer new and uncharted; a body of practice has been developed through the demonstration which can be applied on a larger scale; finally, the demonstration, because of its relative success, may have won some advocates, some support, some desire for its expansion, and some trained cadre.

However, the transition from the demonstration to large-scale institutional change raises a number of managerial issues which are typically ignored and to which the demonstration itself offers no solutions.[6] It is often assumed that the good idea

6. Demonstrations essentially have two potential functions for systems: If they are kept isolated, narrow, and small, they can be used as showcases, en-

or good practice will be disseminated naturally, or sometimes it is mandated by a specific edict or legislation with little consideration of the special processes necessary to institute the idea on a large scale. Surprisingly, there seems little awareness that in actual practice a powerful tendency exists for the original idea to be watered down and vulgarized.

From a managerial perspective two features must be considered at the outset. First, it must be recognized that the demonstration will not be applied equally everywhere. Special methods must be introduced to compensate for the watering-down tendency and, if possible, to reverse this tendency. Second, a strong effort should be made to improve upon the results found in the demonstration as new information is gathered and hopefully codified from a variety of new situations, and particularly from model sites that can be established. If we recognize the limits of the demonstration, it should be possible to improve greatly on the demonstration findings when conscious attention is directed toward this objective and the necessary practices are instituted. The second point that is made above—that demonstration results should be improved upon as new information becomes available—can provide powerful medicine for compensating and even reversing the watering-down tendency that is inherent in instituting large-system change.

PROPOSED METHODOLOGY

Following are some of the steps and specific practices that might be useful in applying an effective practice on a large scale.

1. It is necessary to specify clearly the goals and objectives of the proposed change and to establish a timetable for achieving these goals. This will prevent both grandiosity and disillusionment and enable the change agent to assess clearly what is happening and make appropriate corrections.

---

abling the system, whether it be education or any other, to maintain its business as usual. In some cases, the demonstration may be relatively large, constituting a parallel system, but still enabling the main system to maintain its stability. The other, more positive function of the demonstration is to provide a mechanism whereby a system that is in trouble can be reformed by utilizing the findings and processes of the demonstration. It is to this agenda that this chapter is directed.

2. An aspect of point one is "planned phasing"—that is, moving from the experimental demonstration to ever larger territory in carefully planned steps, rather than attempting to institute a new practice into the entire system at once. Phasing has a number of clear-cut advantages: it allows the idea to spread among those who are more receptive to it and perhaps more likely to institute it well; it develops experience in introducing the idea or practice in relatively large systems and produces a body of practical information that can be useful to large systems; it enables the recruitment and development of a cadre that can then be useful in spreading the idea; it is more manageable and allows for easier feedback and modification—and potential enrichment—of the idea; it leads to the development of a constituency supporting the practice.

   Some relatively successful examples of this phasing, in the development of what might be called a middle-level demonstration, are the U.S. Office of Education's Career Opportunities Program and the Youth Tutoring Youth program. Both programs have been instituted on a fairly small scale, if one thinks in terms of total system change, but a scale that is large compared to the usual demonstration. COP has been established for over 13,000 paraprofessionals in 133 school systems, and the Youth Tutoring Youth program is now in place in over 400 school systems. The same phasing concept, of course, should be utilized in introducing an idea within any school system; thus teachers who are interested in a new idea volunteer to test it, and then the idea spreads to a larger and larger number of teachers.

3. Model demonstration training sites should be established to develop the educational practice and to train personnel. These demonstration training bases should be well funded and equipped to evaluate the practice, develop it more fully, and disseminate the results rapidly throughout the system via conferences, newsletters, and most importantly, workers from other systems who have been trained at the demonstration site. The training base should also provide ongoing technical assistance to projects around the country and should receive information from these projects concerning effective and ineffective methods.

4. An ethos should be built up around the practice—and this has been the case in each of the successful examples already cited —which emphasizes the importance and value of the practice even beyond its specific presumed efficiency. For example,

youth-tutoring-youth programs do more than improve the learning of children; they also increase cooperation and develop the power, resourcefulness, and creativity of children. These results give the program a much larger social meaning, which captures attention, wins a constituency even beyond the immediate users of the program, and may even gain legislative support and media attention. These elements give the program drive and prominence, and in many ways probably increase the motivation of the youngsters, teachers, administrators, and parents who are involved. This climate can help to keep the program growing and can provide the enthusiasm that is such an important ingredient in the experimental demonstration phase. This ethos is nurtured by developing a sense of mission and by media attention, particularly when it takes such forms as filming of the model demonstration program, visits to the program, conferences about it, and articles and books that deal with the concrete and specific as well as the ideological and broad-range implications of the program.

5. Depth training of cadre is an extremely important part of the implementation of a large-scale program. This training can be done at the model demonstration centers, at the work site itself, or in special intensive conferences where specific work problems are carefully simulated and the cadre is "overtrained" in ways of dealing with these problems and issues. It is extremely important to train school principals, administrators, and members of community boards as well as teachers and the specific program supervisors. In the Youth Tutoring Youth model, school superintendents, administrators, and program supervisors are particularly trained. In COP, a major concern has been the training of school principals and community advisory boards. It is extremely important to involve the consumers of the service—that is, the pupils, their parents, and to some extent the advisory boards. The consumer is a key agent of change and a major factor in the productivity of a service.[7]

There are a number of other points about large-scale methodology which should be mentioned briefly: good administrative practice requires that there be someone clearly in charge of the program at the local level and in the large-scale effort who has no other conflicting responsibilities; expediters, trou-

7. See Alan Gartner and Frank Riessman, "New Training for New Services," *Social Work* 17, no. 16 (November 1972): 55–63.

bleshooters, or educational change agents should be dispatched quickly throughout the country to assess difficulties that can be corrected (to some extent this can be done through means of telephone conference calls and videotapes); a strong effort must be developed by the national leadership to fight competitiveness, divisiveness, and small vested interests that could hurt the program; benefits must be found for a great variety of groups for the program; sufficient resources, particularly discretionary funds, must be provided; conferences and other strategies must be used to evoke powerful commitment and participation from everyone whose ideas are considered; a major concentration of effort is crucial so that the program is not diffused by too many different dimensions; small groups or teams of change agents should be introduced at every level to ensure a "critical mass" and to provide the necessary mutual reinforcement and monitoring.

THE YTY EXAMPLE

The Youth Tutoring Youth program suggests a number of ways to prevent atrophy by bureaucratization and to ensure a positive, expanding institutionalization of the program.[8] In essence, the YTY approach depends upon five basic principles:

1. A carefully developed internship program as well as refresher courses for administrators, supervisors, and other personnel.
2. The development of materials for use by supervisors, administrators, and tutors themselves.
3. The winning of a solid commitment from the administrators of the program.
4. The careful assignment of specific people who have as their sole responsibility the carrying out of the program at the local level.
5. The encouragement of flexible modification of the YTY design to make it applicable to specific local conditions.

SUMMARY

A successful transition to a large-scale program requires capturing and using some of the features that characterize the

8. See Alan Gartner, Mary Conway Kohler, and Frank Riessman, *Children Teach Children: Learning by Teaching* (New York: Harper & Row, 1971), especially chapter 4.

demonstration project: "esprit de corps"; flexible application of rules and procedures; zeroing in on the objectives of the program to the exclusion of all the various interferences or distractions that characterize school culture; strong leadership and the designation of specific personnel to take charge of the program rather than assigning responsibility to people who have other responsibilities. In addition to capturing the positive features of the demonstration, large-scale institutionalization of a reform requires a number of other managerial strategies to prevent the watering down of the practice: careful phasing, in-depth training of cadre, the use of model demonstration training sites, the development of a program ethos, and a managerial perspective that integrates the need to develop participation, autonomy, decentralization, flexibility, and openness to the new with the obligation to ascertain that the program is carried through efficiently, in a well-coordinated fashion, and with quality control.

The moving of an idea or a program to large-scale application consists of much more than idea dissemination, for it involves change of the organization and the system. The change agents responsible for widespread institutionalization must have some understanding of organizational theory and particularly of the managerial issues mentioned; otherwise, they may have the simplistic notion that merely disseminating the idea will lead to its institutionalization. Such a view will result in cynicism and despair very quickly.

Conclusion:
Integrating Strength-Based
Approaches

In the compensatory educational model, efforts have been directed by theories that stress the deficits of inner-city children and propose to correct these by various compensatory approaches—special reading classes and the like. Without always directly stating as much, these approaches were guided by the implicit assumption that the schools were all right as they were and it was the children who needed to be changed. The sixties demonstrated fairly conclusively the failure of most of these compensatory measures, at least in terms of affecting significant cognitive improvement, no matter how measured.

What are needed are approaches based upon the strengths of the children, such as youth-tutoring-youth programs, where underachieving inner-city high school youngsters tutor elementary school children who are also doing poorly. Here the message is clearly that the high school youngsters have something to give, something to teach; their strengths are used and they are put in a helper role. It is no wonder, then, that in this context their learning improves dramatically and rapidly in a wide variety of areas, not only on achievement tests, not only in the reading that they are giving as part of the tutoring, but in their total educational function in the classroom and outside it. There is a marked improvement in the number of books they read and in their self-concept. It is this type of approach, built on the strengths of the children, that may be much more useful in promoting leaps in their learning.

The key to a real leap in learning is to integrate in a meaningful fashion a variety of strength-based approaches—e.g., various types of contact approaches, children teaching children, paraprofessionals focusing on educational tasks, and so forth. Currently, these approaches are generally used independently of each other and so, while some good results are obtained, few, if any, big leaps in learning take place. By integrating these strength-based models into a large-scale attack, we may be able to achieve major benefits not only in the learning of inner-city children but in their total development. The question then is how to integrate these approaches; what are the integrating links or themes, and what are the goals?

If we are concerned about education as a route to social change, and if we recognize that in present society lifelong learning, both in school and outside school, is likely to continue, then it would seem very important to develop *learning power* in children. This will enable them to learn how to learn from the family, from the community, from continuing education, from the media, from social action, from experience. This learning power will stand them in good stead throughout their lives.

To arrive at the stage in learning where learning is central requires first that the individual be contacted, and this process is typically slow and individualized. Teachers have to be attuned to this orientation and perhaps specialized contact teachers and paraprofessionals can be developed and assigned to this task. But learning how to learn requires more than being contacted. In particular, it requires the development and self-conscious use of the learning styles of the individual. The student must learn his or her own strengths and weaknesses, and how to limit the weaknesses and fully utilize the strengths. Thus I have given considerable attention to the question of developing learning style throughout this book. For example, I have given a detailed report on how learning power is developed in situations where the child plays the tutor or teacher role, as in the children-teaching-children model.

Of course the learner must also acquire many specific skills —research skills, problem-solving skills—which are terribly useful in the development of learning power and in dealing with lifelong learning problems, in and outside school settings. Schools must also help the learner to see the value of knowledge that goes beyond what is immediately relevant and interesting. The learner needs to see the merit in comprehending the structure of a discipline. Unless all educational personnel up to the highest levels are aware of this, there is a danger of capitulating to the contact level, to the child's immediate interest level.

While the goals—e.g., lifelong learning power—are one way of threading together the different approaches offered, it may also be useful to review the basic themes emphasized throughout the book: (1) emphasis on individualization, built through contact approaches and the development of learning styles; (2) a people-oriented approach rather than a machine-oriented one, so the emphasis is on learning through teaching, as with the use of paraprofessionals, rather than an overemphasis on teaching machines, video techniques, and the like (although the latter can be useful); (3) an emphasis on stages in the development of learning, moving from the contact stage to the stage of learning how to learn, developing basic skills, and comprehending the structure of a discipline or subject matter; (4) an emphasis on *organizing* the strength-based practices that work, developing them fully and self-consciously, and using them efficiently (thus the emphasis in Chapter 8 on the principal as an organizing agent and various methods for moving effective demonstration projects toward large-scale institutionalized reforms); and (5) an emphasis on multiple approaches to evaluation rather than standard achievement criteria, although the latter might be used in the total package.

In short, we need schools where children learn how to learn. All children, not only inner-city children, need schools that are well administered, where teachers are enabled to teach, where paraprofessionals are trained in educational roles, where the logistics are managed efficiently, where all children are involved in teaching other children, where multiple styles are encouraged and built upon, where children move through various stages of learning and considerable attention is given to both contact and post-contact stages, and where parents are involved in working in the school and in influencing broad directions of school policy.

What is special about the educational problems of inner-city children is the prevailing ignorance of the children's strengths. An important factor here is the attitudes, as well as the knowledge, of teachers and other educational personnel. The most obviously destructive attitude is that "inner-city children are incapable of learning, so why bother even trying to teach them." A more benign version is that "since these children have so many environmental problems and so many difficulties in learning, we must not set educational standards, we must be easy on them." Both attitudes result in nonlearning and reveal a lack of awareness of the coping strengths of inner-city children, particularly their resiliency and their sensitivity to other people's attitudes. More important than specific techniques and programs is the need for all educational personnel to understand the strengths of the inner-city child and to build upon these strengths.

Finally, it should be noted that the basic approaches stressed throughout this book, such as the intensive use of paraprofessionals and the use of children as teaching resources, are *cost-saving*. This is highly critical in a society where it is becoming increasingly evident that our resources are not infinite, even were they to be reallocated so that human service work received more support and energy-reducing expenditures less.

Index